# BEREOLAESQUE
## THE CONTEMPORARY GENTLEMAN & ETIQUETTE BOOK FOR THE URBAN SOPHISTICATE

*Composed by*

Enitan O. Bereola, II

authorHOUSE®

AuthorHouse™
1663 Liberty Drive, Suite 200
Bloomington, IN 47403
www.authorhouse.com
Phone: 1-800-839-8640

First published by AuthorHouse 3/2/2009

ISBN: 978-1-4389-3859-2 (sc)
ISBN: 978-1-4389-3860-8 (hc)

Printed in the United States of America
Bloomington, Indiana

This book is printed on acid-free paper.

# WHAT IMPORTANT PEOPLE
## ARE SAYING ...

"Class is subconscious. Style is inherited. Bespoke is a state of mind. The commonality is that they are all in choice. This book teaches you to be exceptional in every way."

Kenny Burns
Lifestyle Specialist/Celebrity Personality
*Former VP of* **Roc-A-Fella Records**
Co-Founder of *RyanKenny*, 1st black designers featured in **Saks Fifth Avenue** since 1980s

"Bereola is the consummate urban sophisticate. His newest release *BEREOLAESQUE* takes a man on a journey to personal and social refinement. He leaves no stone unturned as he answers the  question of the relevance of the modern gentleman.  It is a must read for men of style or those  on a quest to become one, "Bereolaesquely" speaking of course!"

Alex O. Ellis
Author, *Restoring the Male Image*
Founder, *Tied To Greatness*

"This book is like the father or big brother to all those who don't have etiquette or style, but want it and long to learn it. It will instruct them to be simple yet fresh, seen but mysterious."

Aaron Arnold
CEO, *Music Is My Business*
Former member of Sean "**Diddy**" Combs' executive team
"**CNN** deemed Aaron 'Diddy 2.0' because of his style"


"**Brilliant!**"

J.Dakar
Political & Commentary Contributor, **Concrete Loop**
No. 1 Urban Lifestyle & Entertainment blog on the web
Top 50 websites of 2008, **TIME** magazine


"**Man to watch for 2009!!**"

Clutch Magazine
January 2009

# BEREOLAESQUE

## [Be•re•o•la•esque]
### -adjective:

1. Highly appealing and pleasing to the human senses and/or mind; captivating; providing pleasure or delight, especially in appearance or manner; charming, alluring, attractive.

"There is hope for that race or nation that respects its women." -Sutton E. Griggs, *Imperium in Imperio*

To

## Luther Jackson,

*who set the standard for gentlemen long before I came ...*

To

## Rev. Olu Bereola,

*who instilled in me what it means to be charming; alluring; attractive ...*
*all while giving God the honor, the glory, and the praise!*

To

## T. Taylor,

*couldn't help me finish the painting now that you're gone,*
*but the team has been working hard and strong*
*it turned out to be a masterpiece, though some of the paint spilled*
*I'll ensure your legacy is completed and our picture revealed ...*

To

## LVB,

*...thank you for you*

*"I have but the simplest taste ... I'm always satisfied with the best"*

—Oscar Wilde

**This Book Is to Be Judged by Its Cover**

"... I am well dressed, well read, well groomed, well behaved, and well paid. I know the best restaurants and sexiest shops. I symbolize the art of etiquette. I love culture and perfectly aged wine. I am confident and adventurous. If you are smart enough to read me, understand me, and listen to my advice, I will help you get the sexy, the success, the respect, and the lady ..."

... I am BEREOLAESQUE

## READER DISCLAIMER

The content of this book is exclusively intended for the entity to whom it is addressed. I specifically had you in mind when constructing its invaluable scribing. This book contains confidential or privileged material to be used for the benevolence of mankind. Any unauthorized behavior is prohibited beyond this point. I leave you with the responsibility of transforming literature into lifestyle impacting this world one gentleman at a time. For this is not merely a book—but a lifestyle!

—*Keep It Bereolaesque!*

*Final Words from a Contemporary Gentleman …*

# Contents

*Prelude*

## *Prelude*

*An avid connoisseur of sexy ... rurally raised, yet metropolitan minded. A casual author, an introverted artist, and somewhat of a perfectionist in all realms. Learning lessons but staying honest. Because I'm shameless, I'm an open book, and because I'm sharp, I'm self-restrained. Spontaneous but always rational. Humble but quite often ostentatious. I come off as a walking, talking dichotomy, which makes me absolutely Bereolaesque, just like you.*

This book is for ...

... the relaxed, the humble, the verbose, and the poised—this book is for you. The rude, the ignorant, the uninformed, and the shameless—this book is for you. The sexy, the successful, the humble and the creative—this book is for you. Whatever path of life you walk; this book is intended for you. This book was developed with a purpose and this book is for every man—*and woman*—who wishes to live life with a purpose.

Capture its wisdom ... bask in its good word ... adhere to its value ... laugh at its sarcasm ... reflect on its reason ... appreciate its uniqueness ... think of its relevance ... and promote its truth.

Enjoy with candlelight and a friend ...

Without further ado—I give you, *Bereolaesque.*

*The Diagnosis*

# The Diagnosis: *Member Orientation*

1   *A gentleman must abstain from being sexually interesting or risqué*
2   *A gentleman must never be spontaneous, but always plan accordingly*
3   *A gentleman refrains from swearing at all times*
4   *A gentleman must remove his hat when in-doors*
… *Blah, blah, blah (circa, the past)*

## … THAT IS EXACTLY WHAT THIS BOOK IS *NOT* ABOUT!

**This book is about being sexy, successful, contemporary, and comfortable in your own skin!**

Just in case you forgot, I'm here to remind you that the past was decades ago. The times of traditional suits and conservative haircuts are buried with the people who wore them.

Urban sophistication comes in all shapes, sizes, and colors—and the contemporary gentleman looks a lot like you, nothing like me, and everything in between. My vision is to offer you a highly appealing lifestyle with class and distinction in exchange for normalcy. My goal is to educate and uplift you, while exposing the gentleman within you, no matter how far hidden. My hope is to make the world just a little bit more Bereolaesque, one gentleman at a time!

The concept of the Urban Sophisticate is a complex one in modern society. What are his essential characteristics and how long does it take to become one? What are the moral components associated with being a gentleman? Is it still necessary that I lay my jacket down for a woman who has personal assistants to walk over a puddle? That old lady who used to need help crossing the street just drove past me in a Hummer. Is the gentleman still relevant?

How can one be taken seriously in the business world with pleases and thank yous? A butler with a briefcase is a bad idea! You might ask yourself, who courts women nowadays? What can chivalry do for me? Showing up with flowers and holding doors open seems a bit "last season." Why should I adhere to outdated standards and practices when all I have to do is buy a woman a drink to get what I want from her?

This raises the compelling the question—why should I have manners when the rest of the world doesn't? How will good behavior beget a good promotion, or increasing etiquette increase my equity? Are these not valid questions? But of course they are—these are the questions that challenge a gentleman's relevance.

In the past, life has offered us one of two options—cool or corny, with not much in between. Often times the cool were the bad guys and the cornballs were the good guys.

Most would argue that one can't keep it cool and sexy while preserving the purpose and prestige of a true gentleman; it's an oxymoron, like bad sex. Your clothes are too stiff and hard to move in and your suspenders are lifting your pants too high. You're too focused on the stock market exponentially falling to notice your swagger is also drastically falling.

In the Victorian era, British aristocrats believed that gentlemen were gentlemen by right of birth. Industrial and mercantile elites designated themselves as gentlemen according to their wealth and influence. Members of Parliament were recognized as gentlemen by virtue of their occupations. Eventually they all agreed that the recipient of a liberal education at one of the elite public schools begot a true gentleman. They were all wrong; any man can be a gentleman. For the reader of this very book produces the finest gentleman indeed!

Some suggest chivalry is dead and being a gentleman is a thing of the past. I would argue that chivalry is not dead … it has been lost in time, and at completion of this book, will enjoy its anticipated release. In stark contrast to the negative images we are bombarded with in the media and in our very own communities and homes, the new gentleman is refreshingly retro, reminding us of what a man should be.

I am not suggesting that men should be corny, walking around in suspenders and bow ties daily; however, some basic good manners will go a long way in helping you during your ascent to the top. This book introduces new ideas and opens up the mind to a lifestyle that will ensure achievement in every walk of life. Follow these simple tips, and I can assure you will be perceived as a man of good breeding and taste—hence a man people wish to associate and conduct business with, socialize and schmooze with, and handover their courtside tickets to when out of the country on business. Not to mention the fact that the ladies are always quite pleased to meet a real gentleman!

This is a gentleman and etiquette book for the Urban Sophisticate. You might be asking yourself, "What the hell is an Urban Sophisticate?" Well, it is you, it is me, it is anyone with class, taste, morals, and goals—anyone who strives to better himself in every possible way but who is also hip, funky, classic, and of course, fly!

The transition from boyhood to manhood and everything in between and beyond can be quite tricky. There is no set manual to adhere to, and we did not all grow up with father figures or positive role models. Even some of us who have had the blessing of a father present still do not get it! We graduate from childhood, matriculate through life, and move to major cities to find great jobs … but we still do not get it.

I know life gets tough, so I have made life's journey easier for you. The lifestyle that this book creates will lead to success stories, promotions, increased social circles, and an overall appreciation for yourself and life! It has also been said to lead to an increase in childbirth—married, of course!

**The conclusion has been reached:** As long as there exists man and woman, the gentleman will remain relevant—the difference is society. Times have changed and so have people. Women are CEOs, presidential candidates, and so much more. We live in an era where most women have evolved and become more independent, while most men have regressed and become much less dependable. The other half of men have become less cultivated—more average, less desirable, more promiscuous—less distinguished, and more of the same. The diagnosis is in, but despite these staggering statistics, the cool is around the corner; now cometh the time to redefine it.

*The Cure*

# The Cure to the Common Man: *Bereolaesque*

## THE DEFINITION

*BEREOLAESQUE* [Be-re-o-la-esque]—adjective: Highly appealing and pleasing to the human senses and/or mind; captivating; providing pleasure or delight, especially in appearance or manner; charming, alluring, attractive. Example: The dim lighting, mellow music, and sexy decor made for a Bereolaesque atmosphere.

*"My father always stressed the importance of the family name. It is a name worn by kings and chiefs to be held in high regard commanding great honor!"*

Here lies the key to an extraordinary lifestyle. This is by no means an attempt to create clones, but to provide the framework to becoming Bereolaesque. You might be asking yourself, "What in the hell is Bereolaesque?" First and foremost, Bereolaesque is the way you walk—confident; the way you talk—unequivocally; the things you say—clearly; and how you say them—unmistakably! Bereolaesque is how you write

7

and what you write, how you dress, how you smell, what you eat, and where you go! It is how you view yourself and how the outside world views you—it is how people treat you and how you treat others. Secondly, you want everything to do with it!

**A lot of women think that they can only get excitement from a bad boy.**

The contemporary gentleman has arrived! The Bereolaesque man possesses an edge—his own uniqueness that sets him apart from others; he is the uncommon man. He is polished. Most importantly, he is especially mannerly. Bereolaesque is a universal language, and upon completion of this book, Bereolaesque will best describe you!

**Being Bereolaesque makes having manners sexy.**

*"My mother always stressed the importance of conducting myself in accordance with my family name, having great manners, and remembering to always keep it gentlemanly. Following this advice has gotten me far in life!"*

The traditional gentleman operated within limits that defined the range of normal behavior. This book allows your paint to fall outside of those traditional lines, all the while remaining classic.

*ETIQUETTE*—n. rules of acceptable behavior. The conventions governing correct or polite behavior in society in general or in a particular social or professional group or situation.

*MANNERS* *separate humans from animals.*

*"Manners maketh man."*
~~William of Wykeham
Motto of Winchester College and New College, Oxford

Etiquette is merely a collection of forms by which all social interactions are made smooth.

Tune in to your local TV stations, take a stride downtown, or even head over to your place of employment, and you will be amazed. The standards of behavior in our culture have become so questionable that signs of proper conduct have almost completely vanished. Consider for a moment the idea of "correct behavior." While the rebel in us is immediately skeptical of anything correct, our society is desperately in need of people who understand functional, practical, and well-mannered conduct. As many people don't care to be polite, there are minimal outlets to even begin to know how to be polite. We will change that tendency, elevate standards, and demonstrate good manners and supreme civil conduct during this journey.

We will operate from the concept that excellent behavior—proper etiquette—enhances every level of public and private interaction; therefore, it is not only useful and pleasing but also advantageous to both the practitioner and the people who come into contact with that person. This is our mission—to change the world around us, in small but significant ways, one person at a time. And we begin with you, our reader.

*"No act of kindness that you are able to commit is ever too small."*
~~Remi B.

Significantly, excellent behavior is becoming more necessary in our culture with each passing day. As our society moves away from civilized manners, it slides toward rudeness and ignorance. As our collective behavior degenerates, people become less tolerant, less flexible, more brittle and more impatient. It is all too obvious to state that bad behavior causes ever worse behavior—from the programs we watch to the music we choose to listen to, our society has drunk from the bottle of ignorance and is under the influence of dreadful behavior. The world needs better role models. Gentlemen, we must be careful what we consistently subject ourselves to.

*"Be not deceived; evil communications corrupt good manners."* ~~Corinthians 1:33

Poor behavior must stop. We must make the decision that excellent behavior will promote superior values in this world, and that excellent behavior must begin with each of us. Gentlemen, we have the opportunity change the world, and that change begins with you.

## Reactions Speak Louder Than Words

As men, we live our lives like we are constantly in a game of sports. How many times has our initial reaction to conflict led to immediate retaliation? What is it in us that triggers that so-very-sensitive button that causes us to react and retaliate against our counterpart? Someone disrespects you, disrespect him or her back. Someone harms you, harm him or her back. But if someone honors you, why can't you honor him or her back?

I'm not sure where things got mixed up along the course of time, but this isn't the way of life. Many of us don't practice courtesy, yet we expect and sometimes even demand it. Hypocrisy is at an all time high, gentlemen. Turning the other cheek may sound like a foreign concept, but it is a notion that we must get cozy with. Being Bereolaesque is a lifestyle, not a reaction to something done to you. Putting your best foot forward reflects better on you than putting your best fist forward.

Being a gentleman is something that we must live by and practice daily— even when our feelings or emotions don't agree with it. Gentlemen, remove the ideology of an *eye for an eye*. Redirect the emotion that leads to anger, and swallow your pride. Your pride will drag you down, bring everyone with you, and leave you to wallow in your misery alone. If you don't believe me, choose your pride over your girlfriend and see where it leaves you. This being the case, why do we choose pride over our morals, relationships, careers, families, and our very own souls? Holding on to pride is like holding on to acid—it will burn and eventually destroy you. Let it go, gentlemen. Let it go!

## How We Treat Others Affects How We Are Treated

Many people don't realize that karma will always find them, no matter how fast they run or where they hide. The way we treat others is, in fact, the way we are treating ourselves. You may ask how this is possible. Everything comes back full circle, and what we put out eventually comes back to us. Keep this philosophy in mind before keying that car, punching that guy, or cheating on that woman.

## We Are Already Experts at Bad Behavior

Our society already overflows with people who have mastered the art of incorrect behaviors: abysmal expressions, terrible grammar, me-first actions, awful enunciation, garish styles, conspicuous consumption, improper clothing, and rudeness bordering on violence—the list stretches into infinite space. When we get dressed in the morning, we put on our discourtesy first ... it is considered stylish. Not to mention vulgarity is the latest trend—It is not only tolerated but it is embraced.

Consider the notion of polite, refined conversation. It is substantially simpler to converse with a polite person because that person has the tendency to put you at ease through their behavior. You not only enjoy chatting with that person but you actually pay attention to what they say. Courteous behavior is respectful behavior. This is a particularly sore subject for some businesspeople. You know the type of person—they truly believe the only way they can "get results" is to shout at the people around them. They use hostility as a motivational tool. Of course, this is childish behavior at best, assuming that threats are the only thing to which people will respond. As you know, hostility and threatening behavior will only have an effect for a short time. People adjust. They get used to hearing the threats and screaming, and they simply shut it out. The only time we talk to people is when we are punishing or criticizing them. You have to earn the right to criticize someone. We must focus on lifting people up and finding the positive in them. Only then will our criticism be heard. *"Rudeness is the weak man's imitation of strength."* ~~Eric Hoffer

On the other hand, polite behavior does not just show respect for other people, it is also an invitation to each other, an attitude that is attractive by definition. Excellent manners demonstrates the faith one person has in others; it shows that we care for each other. *"To have respect for ourselves guides our morals; and to have deference for others governs our manners."*
~~Lawrence Stern

## The Advantages of Excellent Manners

The presence of so much rudeness can actually benefit the gentleman—because the world's standards have sunk so low, never has it been easier to make an excellent impression. When meeting that special lady, networking, or even being considered for a job, it is easiest to stand out when being mannerly and keeping it Bereolaesque!

## The Faith of Good Manners

Excellent behavior, in addition to being a lifestyle, is also a faith. As religions demonstrate behaviors that are morally and spiritually effective, etiquette teaches us behaviors that are respectful of ourselves and the people around us. It is no stretch to suggest that proper manners are the Golden Rule of public behavior: *Do unto others as you would have them do unto you.* In the pursuit of excellent etiquette, we take the Golden Rule a step further: *Do unto others better than you would have them do unto you.* This is a triple whammy (something like killing three birds with one stone)—you store up good karma for yourself, it has a domino effect, and most importantly, it is pleasing in the eyes of God.

If anything is certain, our behavior forms the basis by which we are judged and revered or damned and reviled. It is axiomatic—if one wishes to form an excellent impression, one must behave with excellence. The practical reasoning behind superior manners becomes obvious—if one wishes to achieve one's goal, one must behave in a way to attain it.

*"Good manners will open doors that the best education cannot."*
~~Clarence Thomas

Be good.

*The Man in the Mirror*

# The Man in the Mirror: *Assessment*
## Inclusively Exclusive: Setting the Standard

*"Perception is reality ..."*

Scientific research has long demonstrated the power of suggestion in perception as well as the strong effects of expectancies. If you dress up an ass and throw rags on a genius, the ass is likely to have more opportunities in life than the genius ever will. Some of us are so comfortable with our own perception that we begin projecting it over our reality. It is much easier to take the credit for being someone else than to endure the hard work toward actually becoming that person. Come on, men, we're all guilty of acting like someone we desire to be, but haven't quite arrived at being. Now, I am not suggesting that having a role model is wrong, but how many times have you—*ladies reading*—heard a guy (especially in L.A. or New York) claim to be an actor, but was actually an unpaid extra in an unreleased film? It is okay to dream, but even sexier to live out those dreams!

All of us men must face a time in our lives when we must come to grips with who we are and how others define us as a person. This can be a very sensitive subject. Generally, dealing with reality is not easy. Many of us either ignore or prolong this inevitable meeting in the mirror, but gentlemen, the time is now!

17

Being Bereolaesque requires us to constantly look in the mirror ... not the tangible glass mirror, but the one that reflects our soul and the true essence of who we are. Before the quest to being Bereolaesque can begin, this self-assessment and reflection must take place. Get into a position of solitude and engage in whatever your vice is in order to clear your mind—nothing illegal, of course! You must ask yourself, "Who am I?" Be careful not to let your reflection answer that question for you. Some of us allow the image of who we are perceived to be define who we are. We become so wrapped in our image that we fail to realize who we really are; we become completely lost. At this point, we are more comfortable living as our image—*alter ego*—than accepting our own realities.

We've all heard the phrase *reality bites!* There have even been films and songs promoting this very ideology. Realize reality is not such a bad thing when it can be altered! It's okay that you're thirty-three years old and still haven't started life's goals—thirty's the new twenty! It's okay that you buy the most expensive clothes but you're late on your mortgage! I'm not blaming you for life's addictions. It is okay that you tell people you own an expensive home but you're living in your Maybach Mercedes Benz. All of these scenarios are okay because they can all be changed! Don't make an ass out of yourself. Leave the "**ass**" inside of "**ass**essment." This is not your lifestyle. It is important, as a gentleman, to always project your best image, but that image must coincide with who you really are as a man.

A true gentleman does not put up any type of front. You are who you are because you do what you say. If you are taking a course in biology pre-medicine, you are not a doctor yet … but you will be if you continue working hard at it. Be true to who you are and even truer to who you desire to become. *Bereolaesque* started as a thought and flourished into the very book you are reading today. Hard work, dedication, and prayer will get you anywhere you want to be, so be encouraged. Don't settle for just looking good on paper.

**Remember that humility is a large part of being Bereolaesque. But being humble doesn't mean you can't be your best, look your best and act your best. Just keep it all in perspective … keep it Bereolaesque, gentlemen, and put your best foot forward! We all want the man in the mirror to reflect the man that we really are.**

*Interlude*
*Sound*

# Speaker Box

This word bank serves as a cheat sheet for gentlemen. These key words are to be a part of the gentleman's vernacular at all times:

## When to Say …

+ **Please**—anytime you ask for or command something.

+ **May I**—anytime you request permission.

+ **Thank You**—anytime you receive something.

+ **No, Thank You**—anytime you do not wish to receive something.

+ **Sir**—when addressing a superior or someone old enough to be your father (until told otherwise). If you are over thirty, it is appropriate to refer to him by his title followed by the last name.

+ **Madam/Ma'am**—when addressing a distinguished woman or a woman old enough to be your mother. If you are over thirty, it is appropriate to refer to her by her title followed by her last name—Be aware that some women find Madam/Ma'am to be disrespectful; do use discretion

   > **In reality, sometimes titles do not even matter. Some folks are laid-back while others are more formal. It is okay to ask someone how he or she wants to be addressed. However, in Southern culture, it is appropriate to use sir and ma'am addressing an elder out of tradition, humility, and respect.

+ **Excuse/Pardon Me**—when walking in between people or in someone's personal space, leaving a room/dinner table, farting, burping, sneezing, clearing throat, yawning, grabbing for attention, and any form of clarification or interruption.

+ **Bless You**—when someone sneezes.

+ **How Are You?**—some folks will mistake you for their therapist, so only ask if you truly care to know.

+ **Pleasure To Meet You**—when introduced to someone new.

- **Goodness**—when she is sexy.

- **Shall We?**—when she is beautiful.

- **Will You Marry Me?**—when she is Bereolaesque!

**I Want A Divorce**—when she is no longer Bereolaesque (no, really avoid divorce at

all costs. Marriage is a sacred union under God that should not be broken).

## The Blueprint

# The Blueprint: *Gentleman Effortlessly*

Being a gentleman is an effortless act. To be one, you must first understand one. A gentleman operates off the basic philosophy of service—the offering up of oneself in order to benefit another is what being a gentleman is all about. **Service is sexy!**

The practice of making yourself useful may take some getting used to, but will quickly become a natural gesture. They say practice makes perfect, yet there is no such thing as human perfection … but there is such a thing as Bereolaesque. Following these basic guidelines to manners should have you on your way to becoming quite the Bereolaesque gentleman … and that is near perfection, right? Of course it is!

*-Disrespecting life's* **little** *rules can result in* **big** *consequences.*

## RULE # 0

### Start With the Golden Rule

Many of us men have our priorities "dyslexic-ally arranged." We treat others like we *don't* like to be treated ourselves—we demand respect and want power but aren't willing to do what it takes to earn it. It is *nice* to be important, but more important to be *nice!*

## Treat others like you want to be treated. You
have heard this phrase time and time again. It probably has little meaning to you at this point. This simple mindset will get you further in life than you would ever imagine. Of course the Golden Rule assumes that you want to be treated kindly and with respect. Let us revisit this ancient proverb. Human nature states that from birth and throughout the rest of our lives, we all want to be loved, no matter how tough our skin is. Why do you think we as men are angered when a significant other is unfaithful? Or when we act out in irrational rage? The essence of it all is us yearning to be loved. The majority of violent people are violent because they are screaming for love. The best way to receive that love is to put out that love; a gentleman reaps what he sows!

## RULE # 11

### Diminish Violence

We offer the idea that instilling good manners and proper behavior will have the effect of reducing the potential for frustration, perhaps even diminishing violence in our culture. Consider a typical incident of rude behavior—a rude driver cuts off another car. While the first action of rudeness is typical, an equally rude response can actually be dangerous. Chasing down the first car and cutting it off might lead to a more significantly violent exchange.

Consider another typical incident of rude behavior: a man steps on your brand-new shoes at a nightclub or looks at your girlfriend a little too long for your liking. Your reaction can either defuse the situation or leave somebody twitching on the floor. I don't mean to sound alarming, but it is just the nature of the world today.

These scenarios can easily be avoided by displaying some basic manners. This may not sit well with the "tough guy" in you, who is accustomed to reacting in these situations, but I've got news for you—tough guys die too. Common sense plays a great factor in the role of a gentleman. In essence, the more gentlemen that exist, the less violent the world we live in!

## RULE # 22

### Kindness

Do away with the notion that kindness is for those who are not beautiful, brilliant, courageous, or strong. Popular culture often associates kindness with being extra gentle, overly sensitive, and/or vulnerable. Popular culture also suggests that having the number-one movie excuses drunk driving. It further suggests that being born to a wealthy family justifies inexcusable behavior. To hell with pop culture—we will all be kind.

The ability to offer something to someone satisfies our natural being with a sense of joy. Giving is an effortless fulfillment that benefits both parties involved. Although we have become independent, too busy, and in a hurry, the least we can do is offer someone in need a helping hand.

Stop to give that person directions; provide a nice compliment for once; if you see a woman struggling to do something, be kind— genuinely offer your assistance to her with no ulterior motives. Don't flirt with her while you help change her flat tire ... unless she really is that sexy—No, really, it is acceptable to flirt back if she flirts first. You never know, she just might be "the one." Just remember to remain genuine in your kindness.

Do use discretion, as our world is becoming more violent—do not pick up hitchhikers or strangers. Use good judgment and do not allow people mistake your kindness for weakness.

## RULE # 33

### Generosity

Etiquette is a selfless expression; always keep others in mind. When a gentleman pulls out food, gum, candy, etc. in the company of others, it is in good conduct to offer some. If you do not wish to share, be discreet about it or eat before you arrive.

If someone is in need, a gentleman is the first to help or offer his services; it's responsible; it's sexy! Keep in mind that we are not superheroes and cannot save the world; devote time to yourself as well.

## RULE # 44

### Consideration

One cannot classify himself a gentleman without possessing consideration. Being considerate is one of the most basic rules of etiquette/manners. Consideration involves concern for the perceptions and feelings of others and the intention not to offend. This includes remaining quiet in places that do not require a soundtrack courtesy of you (movie theater/bookstore/library/coffee lounge)—including cell phones. Be aware of what is not expected or desired in certain environments, such as: pets, babies, or cigarettes. Also respect people's time. Being late isn't sexy in the least bit—fashionably late to the proper venue is the exception—*your place of employment is not that exception.*

## RULE # 55

### Favors

No matter how successful we are, we all serve a greater purpose in life. We need each other to survive, and we all have something to offer one another. The gentleman asks for favors with grace, assurance, and within reason. Refrain from pity fishing to get others to do for you. On the contrary, closed mouths don't get fed, so if you need a favor within reason, ask.

## RULE # 66

### Opening Doors

Normally open doors for ladies, including car doors! Some will thank you and some will not. Do not allow unappreciative folk to kill your kindness. However, in the professional/business atmosphere, opening doors may offend a woman. Use discretion, but remember it is always better to be courteous than to be rude.

## RULE # 77

### Table Etiquette

This art does not necessarily have to be practiced everywhere, but it is important to know for formal dinners, business lunches, or dates.

A gentleman pulls a lady's chair out and adjusts accordingly. Be quick, because most women today have never experienced a true gentleman and will pull out their own chairs. After guests are seated, take your seat last. Elbows on the table are okay when in conversation, waiting for the food. However, when the food arrives, it is mannerly to remove them, to avoid knocking over any utensils. Turn your phone on silent unless the meal is very casual and among good friends. The knife blade should be placed on the edge of your plate when not in use and should always face inward. The salad fork, knife, and soup spoon are further from the main plate than

the main course knife, fork, and spoon. Dessert utensils are either placed above the main plate or served with dessert.

First things first; say a blessing over your meal and wait until everyone has been served to begin eating. Do not place an entire dinner roll into you mouth; break off bite sizes only. It is considered rude to refuse a dish unless you are on a diet or allergic to it. If food is too hot, have a cold beverage with it. On no account spit it out! If you put the food in your mouth, no matter how much you hate it, swallow it. It is rude to take anything out of your mouth that has been put in it, except bones, seeds, etc. At least respect the time a cook has put into ensuring a good meal by eating it (even if it's just a small serving).

If you happen to be the chef, do not experiment with new recipes if strangers will be present—stick with a dish that is familiar. Always thank and praise the preparer of the meal, no matter how good or bad the food is. If it really is that bad, just make a mental note to kindly decline future dining offers from them or offer to prepare the food yourself. If out dining at a restaurant and the food is bad, do not hesitate to discreetly and kindly let the waiter know. Refrain from making a big deal about it. A good rule of thumb is to never insult the one who prepares your food ... trust me!

Follow the pace of your guest(s) and do not finish your meal too soon before or too late after them. Do not *drink* anything with a *spoon.* Unless you are an infant or an ape, do not intentionally play with or make a mess of food. Act like a human and chew with your mouth closed and sit like a man (back straight up). If you are asked a question while eating, do not answer with food in your mouth; signal that your mouth is full and swallow before speaking. Do not slurp your drink. During restroom breaks, place your napkin in your chair to signify that you are returning, and your fork upside down (prongs down), crossing the knife. When finished with your meal, place your napkin to the left of your dinner plate, and your knife (blade turned inward) and fork should be placed beside each other on the plate diagonally from upper left to lower right.

This may sound like a bunch of mumbo-jumbo, but a gentleman who knows how to formally dine is a gentleman with class. When in the privacy of your own home, relax; put your feet up and your hand in your pants! Eat how you wish, but remember, practice makes Bereolaesque!

## RULE # 88

### Sports Fan's Etiquette

Does such a thing exist? Drink beer or soda, slap hands, and go crazy! Have fun being a fan. However, respect your fellow fans and counterparts. Save the potential boxing match for pay-per-view!

## RULE # 99

### Hats Off

Call me crazy, but this tradition is outdated. Its origins date back to men of lesser rank removing whatever headdress or coronet (crown) they had on to show that they were not attempting to challenge or disrespect the king or chieftain of their country. In the age of chivalry, knights in armor lifted their visor to indicate that they were not afraid of being attacked and to give assurance of their peaceful intentions. This has no relevance today. However, I do believe that in places or times of respect and when introduced to elders, it is appropriate for a gentleman to remove his hat. But when hanging with your buddies or just relaxing (whether indoors or not) leave your hat on and chill out—keep it Bereolaesque.

## RULE # 110

### Give Up Your Seat

When a lady or elderly person arrives and there are no available seats, you should stand up and offer yours.

## RULE # 121

### Put on Her Coat/Offer Her Yours

Always help a lady put her coat on or offer her yours if it is cold out. This simple but powerful action is likely to leave you out in the cold, but you're a man ... so take it!

## RULE # 122

### Walking with a Woman

A gentleman always walks along the curbside of the pavement in the company of a woman. This is done in order to protect her from traffic—in other words, you will be the one getting hit by the car! Allow her to walk slightly in front of you, not to check her out from behind, but to offer defense from danger that may be lurking. As gentlemen, one of the most important things we can offer a woman is security! Offer your hand to a woman when she is entering or exiting a platform.

Another point of etiquette is to never leave a woman by herself, even if she is getting on your nerves; not even then. A man never leaves his lady.

A man also refrains from spitting in front of a lady—my mother, a lady with class, hates it and so should you.

## RULE # 133

### Elevators

A gentleman should kindly wait for a woman to enter or exit an elevator before he does. If the elevator is crowded, go ahead and do what you have to do (every man or woman for him- or herself at that point).

## RULE # 144

### Introductions

Introducing guests to one another is a considerate act. Always introduce a gentleman to a lady and follow a deference structure with folks who are your senior. If he is a gentleman, extend your hand for a handshake. This connection can leave a powerful impression. A web-to-web firm handshake—*do not squeeze*—with direct eye contact speaks volumes and sets the stage for a positive encounter. Remember to shake hands during the departure as well.

## RULE # 155

### Art of the Apology

In polite society, an apology is a useful tool and welcome gift. As an act of remorse for a mistake or misstatement, an apology is a sign of concern, respect, and cultured behavior. There are, however, people who misuse apologies or employ apologies as a substitute for other behaviors. Simply put, these misuses are signs of immature or rude behavior. It is important to beware and be wary of the apology. Here are the guidelines for apologies:

## Only When Appropriate

Apologies are useful when a mistake or accident has occurred: stepping on someone's toes, inadvertently cutting in line, dropping a cup, etc. The apology should be heartfelt, clear, and direct. You may offer two thoughts of the following suggestion (but never three):

o   *I'm so sorry*

o   *Please excuse/forgive me*

o    *I apologize for the error*

Turn to face the sufferer(s) of the accident and speak directly to them. An apology offered with your back to the person, or tossed off while you are walking away, is not an actual apology and can be interpreted as an insult.

## Be Specific

*"Forgive me for stepping on your toe"* is not infinitely preferable to *"Hey, sorry."*

## Do Not Apologize When an Apology Is Not Called For

Some people use an apology when they actually want something else. For example, if you cannot hear someone, you should say *"Excuse me?"* rather than *"I'm sorry?"* Remember that an apology is a statement, not a question.

## The Apology Should Fit the Gaffe

If you have complimented a woman on her pregnancy—when she is merely overweight—you should apologize once— quickly—and get on with life. If you have destroyed a friend's car, the apology should be somewhat more substantial. In addition to offering to fix the vehicle, you might consider a note of regret and perhaps an airline ticket somewhere nice. It is important to align the apology with the magnitude of the gaffe.

## The Apology Should Not Be More Substantial than the Gaffe

While it is important to make amends, overly effusive, demonstrative, and/or extravagant apologies will make the sufferer feel even worse. The victim of the gaffe will resent your effusiveness, suspecting that the apology was intended to relieve your guilt rather than to make them feel better. Remember, an apology is for the other person, not for you.—*Empathy diminishes the distance between the accused and the victim.*

## For Small or Medium Blunders, *Apologize Once*

A mistake is a mistake. One mistake gets one apology. If you apologize repeatedly for a single mistake, the sufferer will construe that you are insincere or worse. We all know the complainer who apologizes endlessly over a minor infraction. This person becomes, in the vernacular, a pain in the ass. As we have noted, they are not apologizing as much as they are going through some sort of insecure psychological episode.

## An Apology Is a Bridge, Not a Destination

In polite behavior, an apology is a bridge that allows you to rise above an error, mistake, or blunder. Once you have crossed that bridge, put it behind you and the sufferer. Do not wallow in the moment any longer than comfort and decorum permits.

## RULE # 166

### Sympathy Etiquette

When family, friends, or associates become injured or ill or pass away, it is often difficult to know your proper role. What are you supposed to do or say? Flowers, plants, or cards help say what is often difficult to express. This is why it is always appropriate and in good taste to send an arrangement. It adds warmth and provides the emotional support important to the family. A phone call or visit is appropriate in cases of injury and illness. Deaths can be a different scenario. Everyone grieves differently. A gentleman extends his condolences and makes himself available to the family for support. A phone call or voice message is acceptable (unless advised otherwise by the family). An e-mail or text message is a bit too impersonal for such a situation.

Prayer is most effective in these scenarios.

## RULE # 177

### Respecting Parents/Authority

This may not be the easiest thing to do. It would be foolish to assume that everyone has a pleasant relationship with their mother and father. Despite what may be, respect for your mother and father is in obedience with God's word—at the least, respect them for bringing you into this world.

*"Honor your father and mother. This is the first of the Ten Commandments that ends with a promise. And this is the promise: If you honor your father and mother, you will live a long life, full of blessing."*

~~Ephesians 6:2–3

## RULE # 188

### Appreciation

As gentlemen, appreciation is something that we are very comfortable with. When receiving a kind gesture, whether it is a gift, compliment, or good deed, the gentleman is appreciative. He understands that people do not have to do for him, so when someone extends a kind offering, he humbly accepts with a smile of appreciation. Always say *thank you* and mean it. Follow-up phone calls, e-mails, or thank-you notes or cards are appropriate in situations of meaningful gestures. Taking the time to write a thank-you note is a pleasant deed. It is slightly more personal than a card, so exercise particular judgment when deciding which method to use. Unless you are looking for a date, avoid certain types of flowers or plants, as they may give off the wrong impression in personal or business settings.

## The Right Flowers for the Right Occasions:

**Aster:** daintiness and love; fidelity
**Cactus:** endurance
**Camellia:** admiration and perfection
**Carnation (general):** fascination; love; distinction
**Carnation (red):** deep love and affection
**Carnation (pink):** I'll never forget you; a mother's undying love
**Carnation (green):** for St. Patrick's Day
**Carnation (white):** sweet and lovely; innocence; pure love; good luck
**Cattail:** peace and prosperity
**Chrysanthemum:** for a wonderful friend
**Chrysanthemum (red):** love, good luck and best wishes
**Chrysanthemum (white):** truth
**Chrysanthemum (yellow):** slighted love
**Daffodil:** You're the only one
**Daisy:** innocence; purity; gentleness; loyal love
**Delphinium:** open heart.; ardent attachment
**Gardenia:** for your secret love
**Gladiolus:** remembrance and sincerity
**Heather:** admiration and solitude
**Hyacinth (purple):** I'm sorry; please forgive me
**Hyacinth (pink):** play
**Hyacinth (white):** loveliness; I'll pray for you
**Hydrangea:** thank you for understanding
**Iris:** faith and hope; wisdom and valor; my compliments
**Ivy:** wedded love; fidelity; affection
**Larkspur:** lightness and swiftness
**Lily (general):** purity of the heart
**Lily (calla):** beauty
**Lily (tiger):** wealth

**Lily (white):** innocence and purity; sweetness; majesty

**Lily (yellow):** gratitude
**Lily of the Valley:** return to happiness; humility
**Magnolia:** nobility
**Mistletoe:** kiss me; affection; to surmount difficulties
**Orchid:** love and beauty; refinement and wisdom
**Orchid:** mature charm
**Peony:** happy marriage
**Petunia:** your presence soothes me
**Poppy:** eternal sleep; imagination
**Primrose:** can't live without you
**Rose (bridal):** happy love
**Rose (coral):** desire
**Rose (dark pink):** thankfulness
**Rose (dark crimson):** mourning
**Rose (lavender):** enchantment; love at first sight
**Rose (peach):** modesty
**Rose (orange):** enthusiasm
**Rose (red):** I love you; respect
**Rose (pale pink):** grace, joy and admiration
**Rose (white):** innocence; spiritual love and purity
**Rose (yellow):** joy, gladness and friendship
**Snapdragon:** gracious; protection from evil
**Stock:** bonds of affection; promptness
**Stephanotis:** happiness in marriage or desire to travel
**Sunflower:** power; warmth; nourishment
**Tulip (general):** gift from a perfect lover; love
**Tulip (red):** irresistible love; believe me; declaration of love
**Tulip (yellow):** hopeless love
**Violet:** faithfulness; modesty
**Zinnia (mixed):** thinking of an absent friend

*~~Chrissie Harten, www.thegardener.btinternet.co.uk*

## Example of the *Personal* Thank-you Note:

*Dear (**Recipient**),*

*I enjoyed my time with you (**Date**). It was such a pleasure to see/meet you.*

*Telling you just was not enough, so again I would like to personally thank you for (**Meaningful gesture**). (**Fill in your own personal sentiments**)*

*Again, you definitely did not have to go out of your way and I appreciate it.*

*Thank you (**Recipient**),*

*(Your name)*

## A Few Examples of Meaningful Gestures:

+ Offering one's home

+ Offering one's time

+ Performing a substantial favor

+ Providing a listening ear

+ Any form of invitation

+ Any form of rescue

+ Going above and beyond expectations

It is commendable for a gentleman to provide a thank-you e-mail or phone call upon new employment—make sure it is more professional than personal. Professional etiquette can be quite different from social etiquette.

Example of the *Professional* Thank-you Note:

> **(Recipient name)**,
>
> *I would like to thank you again for taking the time to meet with me this afternoon regarding (**Circumstance**). (**Fill in your specifics**).*
>
> *Again, you definitely did not have to go out of your way and it did not go unnoticed. I*

*look forward to hearing from you soon.*

*Best Regards,*

*(Your signature)*

*(Your name printed)*
*(Title)*

# RULE # 199

## Professional Etiquette

An executive's good manners imply consideration of his customer's interest, his employee's interest, his company's interest, as well as his own.

Unlike a social scene, professional etiquette is genderless. Follow the same basic guidelines, but understand that chivalry does not necessarily belong in the workplace but ethics and manners do.

We are all aware that e-mail, faxes, conference calls, and cell phones can cause confusion in relation to professional etiquette. You have an all-access communication pass to people at all hours of the day, but refrain from abusing it.

## E-mail

It has become so common in the workplace that the transmission of jokes, spam, and personal notes often constitute more of the messages employees receive than actual work-related material. Remember that your e-mail messages are an example of your professional correspondence. Professional correspondence does not include smiley faces.

## Faxes

Faxes should always contain your contact information, date, and number of pages included. They should not be sent unsolicited—they waste the other person's paper and tie up the lines.

## Conference Call Etiquette

This entails introducing all the participants at the beginning of the call so everyone knows who is in attendance. Since you are not able to see other participants' body language and nonverbal clues, you will have to compensate for this disadvantage by communicating very clearly. Be aware of unintentionally interrupting someone or failing to address or include attendees because you can't see them. And finally, don't put anyone on speakerphone until you have asked permission to do so.

## Cell Phones

Cell phones can be a lifesaver for many professionals. Unfortunately, if you are using a cell phone, you are most likely outside your office and may be preoccupied with driving, catching a flight, or some other activity. Be sensitive to the fact that your listener may not be interested in a play-by-play of traffic or the other events you are experiencing during your call. Also, become quite familiar with the silent/vibrate option. Keep the cell in the silent or off position during any important business meeting. Keep it on vibrate when expecting an important call. If the vibrate function is just as loud as the phone ringing, just turn it off and return the call later. Most importantly, save the childish ringtones for those who haven't read my book. First impressions are a female dog!

## Appearance

Gentlemen, the boardroom is not the proper environment to display your personal creativity. You don't eat spaghetti for breakfast, apple pie for lunch, and pancakes for dinner, do you? Well, don't wear your flashy jeans and earrings in the professional world. Your Easter, leisure, and nightclub suits are just not acceptable! Remove your earrings and excessive jewelry (classic watches are fine), lay off the gel and cologne, and arrive clean and ready to conduct business. The professional world is about being sharp and prepared for the job, so look like that is what you came to do! Even take it a step further and dress like you own the company!

Even if you have impeccable social graces, you will inevitably have a professional blunder at some point. When this happens, "Bereolaesque" offers advice: Apologize sincerely without gushing or being too effusive. State your apology like you mean it, and then move on. Making too big an issue of your mistake only magnifies the damage and makes the recipient more uncomfortable—*see Art of the Apology section.*

# The Movement

# The Movement: *Walking & Talking*

While we have established the *need* for the gentleman in our culture, the *practices* of the well-mannered gentleman are firmly rooted in comfortable, natural behavior. In this chapter, we will examine a range of chivalrous codes of conduct for your consideration and most of all, for you to apply and repeat with confidence.

The listed qualities of the gentleman are his essential building blocks that develop character.

## *What a Gentleman Does*

- ## A Gentleman Is On Time

  Being punctual is important, especially in business. Train yourself to wake up early and seize the day—*carpe diem*. Set your clocks back a few minutes earlier to trick yourself into being on time. Sometimes certain elements are out of our control and tardiness is unavoidable. If this is the case, call in advance and apologize to the person(s) waiting.

### ✦ A Gentleman Listens

If there is a single quality that indicates a well-mannered man, it is his ability to *listen*. The quality of an excellent conversationalist is not the one who speaks well; rather, it is the person who *is well-spoken at the right moments*. We shall spend a few precious moments on the art of listening:

> "Sometimes we talk too much and say the wrong things. God gave us two ears and one mouth; we should listen more than we talk."

~~ Frettie Jackson

- ✦ **Actively engage the person**—Turn your attention and body to them. Connect with them through easy and steady eye contact. Please note: This does not mean you should stare at the speaker; you should engage them to the point where *they* feel comfortable. Nod your head in agreement and communicate back to the speaker with your body language.

- ✦ **Stand your ground**—Good listening requires that you be physically comfortable in the activity. Twitching, shifting, yawning, looking away—these are signs you are bored or distracted. They are also clear signs of lack of interest and negative perceptions, instantly communicated to the speaker as a result.

- **Measure your ground**—A good listener remains on the edge of the speaker's comfort zone—inside arm's length is too close. If you are taller, step back slightly so the speaker is not required to crane to keep eye contact. If you are shorter, hold your ground.

- **Listen to understand**—You must be "taking in" the conversation, installing the ideas and thoughts in your consciousness, rather than just waiting to reply.

- **Let the speaker finish**—A gentleman *never* interrupts a speaker (unless for clarification or an emergency of some magnitude). It is not sufficient to simply allow a speaker to finish their thoughts or ideas; a gentleman will encourage a speaker to do so.

- **Be tactful but be truthful**—If a speaker is being rude or insensitive, it is not necessary to remain in the conversation. It is okay to disengage politely and resolutely.

*"Never argue with an idiot. They will drag you down to their level, and then beat you with experience"*
~~ Idoroenyi Amanam

- **Never gossip**—Generally, the contents of a discussion between two or more gentlemen are never to leave the circle of trust. Gentlemen do not gossip, girls do!

## A Gentleman Is Articulate

A person of quality uses a diverse range of words, *but* that person only uses words he understands and can apply accurately. Showing off extravagant expressions has a tendency to alienate people; a refined person employs the right words at the correct time without force. This is something that should be practiced, eventually becoming natural. If it isn't natural, it isn't Bereolaesque. The words we speak illustrate who we are. How we speak should be in line with how we behave. Be kind and tactful in your speech, realizing that there is power in words. Your tone of voice matters. Sometimes it's not what you say, but how you say it! However, what you say and how you say it also affects lives. Words begin with thoughts and are turned into action. Those thoughts and actions are expressed throughout this book ... the actions are up to you.

*"Death and life are in the power in the tongue ... "*

~~Proverbs 15:4

+ A Well-Mannered Person Enunciates

Possessing an excellent vocabulary or offering an interesting point of conversation is useless if people cannot understand what you are saying. Enunciation is the art of pronouncing words clearly and correctly; this is a rapidly disappearing skill. It is okay for slang to be used among a social group of friends. However, knowing when and where to use slang is vital.

+ Slang

Slang is inappropriate in most conservative settings and business environments, depending on the nature of the business. However, being Bereolaesque is all about being current, so don't shy away from the latest sayings. Employ them casually and without force. Don't *try* to be Bereolaesque … be Bereolaesque … it's natural. Knowing slang requires involvement in or access to specific society and ways of life, so stay current!

+ A Gentleman Thinks Before He Speaks

Nearly all mistakes in conversation are a result of not thinking before speaking. People who talk too easily are apt to talk too much, and at times recklessly. Have regard for the recipient of your words. Do not let discussions turn to arguments, and never tell someone that their opinion is wrong; tell them you disagree. Refrain from being boring or boastful. Speak of topics you are well-versed in. Through knowledge alone does one prove one's right to authority. Refrain from repeating the same stories or jokes over and over—they are not funny. Do not be obnoxious ... just keep it Bereolaesque!

+ ## A Refined Person Pursues Intelligence

A person of quality continues to expand his mind by adding words to his personal lexicon—*reading is the best way to accomplish this*. A gentleman should enroll himself in an area of study for higher education or immerse himself into a specific area of interest, challenging him to always learn more.

+ ## A Gentleman Has Self-Control

He controls his urges, temptations, anger, and most importantly himself.

+ ## A Gentleman Is Slow To Anger

Anger is an emotion that causes you to sweat ... gentlemen are too cool for that.

## ✦   A Gentleman Is Forgiving

He generally does not take offense to small matters; he is easygoing.

As God forgives us, a gentleman forgives his wrongdoer. This

does not mean the gentleman is a pushover and does not stand his

ground and command respect.

## ✦   A Gentleman Is Tactful

In the comedy business, tact is defined as "knowing your

audience." This means a gentleman knows, or quickly discerns,

the sensibilities and sensitivities of the people around him. If an

inappropriate comment does drop, apologize at once. It is not

possible to be both tactless and Bereolaesque—tact does not stop

a gentleman from speaking his mind; just choose your words and

actions and approach carefully.  It's all about timing!

## ✦   A Gentleman Sacrifices for His Family

He provides for everyone first—wife, children—and then himself.

## ✦   A Gentleman Is Private

He never discusses private family affairs with anyone outside of his

immediate family.

## The Art of Hospitality

*How to anticipate what people want and get it right the first time:*

Have you ever entered into a situation with little to no expectations, and left with a pleasant experience that caught you by surprise? That's hospitality for you.

Hospitable people are masters at predicting your needs, meeting your wants, and exceeding your expectations. Hospitality is the difference between a three-star and a five-star hotel. It is the reason why people develop loyalty for specific brands. Hospitality can be the difference between a $5 and a $100 tip!

The art of anticipating what people want is simple—place yourself in their shoes for the moment and ask yourself what you would expect. What would it take to meet your own expectations? The answer to that question is part of the equation to great hospitality. The other part of the equation is doing slightly more than what is expected. Superseding your own expectations is the rule to providing sound hospitality.

It is safe to assume that the reader of this book employs a higher level of expectation than average.

# The Cool

# The Cool: *The Style Guide*
## Essentials for Every Gentleman

God gave us an empty **canvas** and provided the paint and brush. It is up to us to fill the paper with vivid colors, painting a captivating **picture**.

### Power of Colors

-**Black** is classic, stylish, and timeless. It is the color of power. It is dominant and has the ability to drown out any of its predecessors. It is the color of choice in fashion, as it appears to make one look thinner.

-**White** is elegant. It is the color of purity and innocence. It is light neutral, and goes with everything.

-**Red** is considered a power color that commands attention. It is extremely passionate and intense. It is sexy; the color of love.

-**Blue** is a dominant yet peaceful color. It is calming and represents *peace and loyalty.*

*-**Green** is refreshing, relaxing, and easy on the eye. It is a favorable color in decor. It represents masculinity and wealth.*

*-**Yellow** is a bold and sexy attention-getter. As the color of happiness and hope, it enhances concentration and focus. When paired with gray … magic happens!*

*-**Purple** is a regal color of kings and queens alike; it is a color of honor and sophistication.*

*-**Brown** is a masculine color. As the color of oak, it is reliable and genuine.*

*Each color unique in its own right, paired with the right combination, can make for quite the Bereolaesque experience!*

The beauty of the world lies in its diverse collection of cultures, experiences, and differences. It is essential for the gentleman to embrace these distinctive affairs, thus providing the option to enhance his own lifestyle. Having these varied abilities makes you a well-rounded man. Women find well-rounded men sexy!

Being Bereolaesque is not an art form achieved from sunrise to sunset. It requires practice and consistency, like any new concept that the brain attempts to soak up and make habit. This chapter provides a guiding principle in matters of artistic beauty and taste. I will considerately assume that I am speaking to the gentleman who knows not a thing about being Bereolaesque. This approach will provide the basic essentials that need to be in every man's possession—that is if you strive to be an appealing gentleman of eclectic aesthetics, providing delight in appearance or manner. I am speaking to the gentleman who strives to be confident, bold, and timeless.

*"Intelligent people are always open to new ideas. In fact, they look for them."*
~~Proverbs 18:15

The same underwear for weeks … dirty clothes … lack of grooming; as men, why do we submit ourselves to these caveman-like standards?

Now, I am not suggesting putting on a dress, hair, and make-up, but a little masculine grooming will go a long way. A gentleman's palate should contain collections that reflect a cultured way of life. This collection of head-turning must-haves oozes sexy, shouts confidence, and proclaims Bereolaesque:

*Style (The Blueprint to Being Bereolaesque):* We all know that person who breezes into a room, immediately commanding the attention of all people in it. He is no supermodel or sexually appealing guy. Hell, half the time he is not one the ladies would deem handsome. What is it about him that freezes time, forcing the attention of everyone around to focus on him? Simply put, style!

A gentleman gets the latest model perhaps, but has it adapted and modified to his own style so that he has just that distinction in appearance. Style is what defines you … it gives you individuality in a climate of redundancy … it is what makes you the yellow in a room of gray … This is what being Bereolaesque is all about! Your style should be unique to your personality. It should be such that when others attempt to duplicate, they fail to measure up.

Your style is the basic defining characteristics of you. Do be cautious not to overdo it—a vulgar style is that which no matter what the fashion of the moment may be, is always too much for the occasion; too exaggerated, or is accessorized out of proportion. People of bad taste are apt to fancy distortions, to exaggerate rather than modify style. This does not mean you cannot express creativity, but only those who are Bereolaesque can pull off that fine balance between creativity and classic style.

A gentleman should walk, talk, and dress with a certain style. He should have a style of conducting business, move with a distinct style, and even have a particular style of thought. Style is something that is completely natural and should never be forced! It is built from experience, and in order to develop style, you must embrace diversity.

**You do not need a stylist to have style.** A gentleman with talent, taste, and originality can be suitably and charmingly dressed on little income each year. The focus is not always on what you purchase, but how you wear it. The Bereolaesque gentleman attracts a lady with just a T-shirt and jeans on—his appeal transcends his garments.

A woman is blinded by style. She is sometimes willing to overlook what you're lacking in the *looks* department if your swagger and style are Bereolaesque!

*For the Mornings—The Polished Gentleman*: The Bereolaesque man should welcome mornings as the start of a new day that God has graciously provided, and appreciate each morning as such. The gentleman always washes his hands after using the restroom and keeps the area cleanly. The gentleman must also have sanitary items that allow for the following:

**clean teeth**—Toothpaste that will fight cavities and tartar; make sure to brush your gums, tongue, and the roof of your mouth as well. Do not forget to floss.

**fresh breath**—Mouthwash that will destroy germs that cause plaque, gingivitis, and that horrible bad breath.

**clean body**—Soap/facial wash that will cleanse your face and body without drying out your skin. Lathering facial wipes are great for the initial cleaning. Next, move on to a facial moisturizer—moisturize your situation without over-drying your sexy. Apply antiperspirant under your arms that won't cause a rash. Avoid antiperspirants that cake up under the arms, staining your garment. Also, a few puffs of baby powder "down there" won't hurt.

**smooth skin**—Invest in lotion that is suitable to your skin type. If you have dry skin, get a lotion that will provide moisture for an extended amount of time, so you will not have to consistently re-apply, wasting time and money. If you have oily skin, you just might not need lotion. If you do decide to use a moisturizer, make sure it is light and non-greasy. Pay close attention to the webs of the hand and the elbows, as they tend to get dry quickly. It would also behoove the gentleman to stray away from lotions with heavy fragrances; most women smell great, but let's leave the sweet lotions to them.

**stylish hair**—Whether sporting a trendy Mohawk or more classic cut, whether you wear your hair short, long, slicked back, or hardly have any hair at all, always keep it fresh. Maintaining haircuts on a need-be basis is essential to being Bereolaesque. Truth is, the way you wear your hair can tell a lot about the person you are. What message do you want to convey? Maintain your facial hair as well; untamed whiskers are for cats and dogs. If you wear a mustache, keep it neatly trimmed and well-kept. An out-of-control mustache reflects an out-of-control life, and the Bereolaesque gentleman has his life under control! The beard is a privilege, as not all gentlemen can grow one. It is a masculine, bold statement of dignity. Do not sport a beard just for the sake of sporting one. Sport yours with pride and with confidence. Just make sure that it is as precisely well-kept as the mustache is. If you decide on the five o'clock shadow, make sure that it is also tamed, despite its unkempt and rough appeal; outline and trim its edges.

**body/nose/ear hair**—Some gentlemen embrace their body hair while others prefer less or no hair at all. If you are married or in a relationship, ask for her preference first before taking matters into your own hands. After all, she is the one who has to see it. However, the gentleman should always maintain or eliminate excess nose and ear hair … it's just not a good look. Skin types react differently to different tools, so know your body—General rule of thumb: if it bumps up on your face, it will probably bump up on your body.

**clean nails**—The gentleman of business and leisure must keep his finger- and toenails under control. Get rid of the dirt, dead skin, and hangnails. Though proper grooming is of major importance, do keep the timing down to a minimum. Do not exceed an hour to an hour and a half. Do not forget, you are indeed a man!


*Messy Sexy:* It's that *woke up and just got out of bed* masculine look that some women can't resist. It reminds her that your sex appeal is effortless, and there are no mirrors required. The magic of this look is that it's solely based on aesthetics—physically attractive gentlemen get away with the look more so than men not too blessed in the *beauty* department. In other words, this look is exclusively for the handsome. Whether heading out to the pool, or on a date, the *Messy Sexy* look is perfect for the summer. This look contrasts well in a tailored suit!

*Common Scents:* The Bereolaesque man should engage in a serious love affair with cologne; he is a connoisseur of it. He has a minimum collection of three fragrances in his possession at all times and should focus on increasing that number. A pleasant smell follows the gentleman wherever he goes. Cologne reacts differently to each skin type, so it does not smell the same on every individual. The best way to find the best fragrance for you is to dedicate a day to sifting through various collections. Visit a fragrance boutique or department store and begin your journey. Like a photograph, the aroma of cologne can capture a point in time. If you want to leave a lasting impression, make a habit of indulging in various colognes. The next time a lady of interest happens to smell your scent on someone else, she will surely think of you—**stay on her mind!**

*-Acqua Di Gio (daytime fragrance), Burberry Touch (afternoon fragrance) and Chanel Egoiste Platinum (evening fragrance) are great beginner collections.*

*\*\*Mixing certain night and daytime fragrances can result in quite the Bereolaesque aroma—try it!*

*Craftsmanship:* Stainless steel and leather should be a part of every gentleman's wardrobe. A gentleman's timepiece is as valuable to him as his time. This one-time purchase is wise investment, so let's not be frugal here. Craftsmanship is key. As most women would have it, shape and size does matter. Pay close attention to precision and detail of a watch: shape, size, metal, technical innovation, bezel, and strap. Remember, this timepiece is timeless.

*-Audemars Piguet is the gentleman's watch of choice for quality and style.*

*For the Noonday:* This is the middle of the day … take advantage of it!

**appointments**—This is the time of day where you get a lot of your business taken care of. Whether it's for work, daily errands, or relaxation, the afternoon should not be taken for granted. Make your callbacks during the afternoons. The gentleman always returns calls in a timely manner.

**exercise**—Sign up at a local gym, go jogging, shot some hoops with the fellows; whatever you do to maintain excellent health, do it in the afternoon (or mornings if you have the time).

*For the Evenings/Weekends:* Loosen up your tie! This is the sexiest time of your twenty-four-hour day, whether you are single, dating, or married. If you had a long day, patronize a local lounge, make reservations at a fine restaurant, or just simply relax with loved ones.

Take advantage of this time to hang out with your kids. You spend enough time maneuvering through the hustle and bustle of the day. Go visit some relatives. Take the family to a movie or bring the movies home to you. Turn the cell phone off and bask in the beauty of your many blessings.

*On a Sexy Date:* Wearing a classy all-black ensemble is a sure way of keeping it Bereolaesque! Do be cautious; sporting all black can be redundant or boring, so this is your opportunity to be creative and keep it funky! Add an uncommon floral piece on the lapel, or even a brooch. Do not go overboard, and keep it as simple as possible—the casual black suit and soft black dress shirt will do. Make sure your blacks do match. When making dinner reservations, stating your first and last name with a heading in front seems to get you seated the fastest. Also, you develop good report frequenting the same establishments. Maintain relationships with the hostess, chef, and owner—hell, even get in good with the security staff. Pick your top three favorite restaurants and pay them visits often. Although they are the ones serving you, do not hesitate to serve them; bring a bottle of wine for the owner—take care of them and they will take care of you!

**<u>Don't forget to tip!</u>**

*Closet:* The gentleman's closet is the doorway to his soul. Your personal views and behavior should be manifested by your outward appearance and style! Businessmen wear suits, athletes wear comfortable sneakers, while relaxed men wear T-shirts and jeans. If you just so happen to be all three, then wear all three. One can stylishly pull this off without being viewed as the oddball; it is the magic of the blazer. When pairing the blazer with just about any top (button-up, T-shirt, V-neck, or sweater), a gentleman can go from boring to stylish in a snap!

By far, the most important garment in a gentleman's closet is not a garment at all ... it is his confidence! Every gentleman should wear his confidence like he wears his underwear—he should put it on before any other article of clothing. Wearing your confidence allows you to wear just about anything you would like. Take, for instance, the incredibly talented Lenny Kravitz, Prince, or Elvis Presley, for that matter. Now, I am not suggesting wearing a skin-tight one-piece, but I am suggesting that their confidence allows them to creatively and expressively wear what they want ... and get away with it! Besides, women around the world find confidence sexy! There's a thin line between confidence and humility. Don't allow your confidence to overshadow your humility and have it mistaken for arrogance—that's not sexy!

The Bereolaesque man is constantly building and updating his wardrobe. At the bare minimum, the gentleman must have the following items in his closet at all times: Enough *fresh underwear* (boxers/briefs, cotton/dress socks, and undershirts) to last you at least three weeks; a quality pair of *dark blue, light blue, and black jeans;* a quality *white dress shirt;* a quality pair of *black and brown dress shoes* with *matching belts; knee-length socks;* at least one pair of *sneakers, shoe cleaning kit, shoe horn, lint remover,* professional *steamer* or *iron* and board, and at least *six sexy suits.*

## Got on My Good Clothes

**Reserved for the Sexy:** The suit is the gentleman's life accessory

*You can get more with a good word and a suit than you can with just a good word ...*

*The Classic Navy Blue:* You cannot go wrong with this suit. Its versatility is a plus. You can wear it to your downtown office or dress it down and casually wear it on a date. It is best paired with a light-colored shirt and darker tie; the double Windsor knot goes great with this suit.

*Calm Gray:* This must-have suit makes a statement; whether subtle or bold, the calm gray suit is sure to make a point. It delivers confidence with a relaxed and humble undertone. Pair it with a light-colored shirt and make a statement with a bold tie. It looks good in wool.

*Sexy Black:* You can never go wrong with the sexy black suit. Whether at the office or on a dinner date, the gentleman adorned in this suit will be appealing. This suit is now seen in a relaxed corporate environment. The slim fit is generally more appealing. Like all your suits, make sure this one is professionally tailored specifically for you. The sexy black suit can be paired with just about any combination of shirts and ties; again, the light shirt and dark-colored tie is a great match.

*The Bold Pinstriped:* This is the suit that exudes extreme confidence. It is bold and daring. You may see the CEO in this suit. The bold pinstriped collection can be found in various colors. You can be traditional or risqué in pairing with this cool suit. From dark or light ties, solid shirts to patterns, the bold pinstriped suit goes well with just about any combination.

*Cool Linen/Cotton/Khaki:* Whichever style you choose, this summery suit should be light in color. It is casually worn (no tie) but the stylish gentleman is able to dress it up. This is the Bereolaesque suit of choice to wear to a social affair, summer wine party, or for an evening off by the water. It is quite Bereolaesque to eliminate socks, throw on some loafers, grab a cigar, and kick back with this sexy ensemble.

*The Classic Tuxedo:* Often referred to as the penguin suit, the classic tux is worn at formal affairs. It is the epitome of a full suit and should be worn with pride, class, and dignity. The classic tux can be paired with a tie, bow tie, and/or cummerbund. Gentlemen, hand-tied bow ties only please! Trust me, it makes a difference. The tuxedo jacket may be casually worn with jeans—mix it up!

**Double-breasted** suits are more of a classic style worn during formal events, but can be casually spiced up—the less buttons, the better.

**Single-breasted** suits are more modern and stylish.

**Three-piece suits** are for either one of the professional collections—these suits add character to the ensemble and provide a distinguished finish. The three-piece can be stylishly worn without a jacket.

Investing in at least one **bespoke** (custom-made) suit is highly recommended. The more bespoke suits the better, but work your way up to it and start off with at least one.

**The slim suit** compliments the gentleman who is in shape. The look is Bereolaesque but definitely not for everyone. The natural shoulder fits the shape of your body; there is no padding. The roped shoulder is a unique classic look that provides a strong visual effect.

## One should not be able to tell the exact contents of your pockets

Leave your bulky personal belongings outside of your suit pockets. They not only compromise the appeal of the suit, but they weigh the ensemble down. Let us not sag our suit pants, gentlemen ... and keep the jewelry to a minimum when a professional suit is worn ... keep it Bereolaesque, sir.

## Do not be afraid to mix it up

The classic top and casual bottom is a good look. Wear half of your formal/casual/relaxed suit up top and jeans/hard-bottom shoes/casual shoes on bottom. Be sure it flows together and wear your confidence with your style.

## Wearing white

Wear it whenever the hell you would like—before or after Labor Day/Easter. We don't follow this outdated rule. Throw on some loafers and grab some white wine, my guys—*grown men only!*

## Know your measurements

Knowing your measurements will make browsing for your perfect suit much easier. Jot them down in your PDA for quick reference.

**Follow the cleaning instructions on the tags of all garments.*

*Suit Accessories:* The bow tie/tie, the tie clip/bar, the cufflinks, the pocket watch (classic/timeless/Bereolaesque), the brooch, the fedora, and the flower pinned to the lapel or in the buttonhole are all extras for the suit. The pocket square/handkerchief is a must-have, and one is never enough. Invest in several colors and styles to accent your suit, blazer, or vest. Wear a different color handkerchief than the color of your tie—take risks! Contrary to popular belief, there is more than one way to stuff that little square into your pocket.

# Five Essential Folds for the Pocket Square/ Handkerchief

- **Mr. Conservative:** This is the most basic kind of fold. It is a simple square-like fold that sits no more than an inch outside of the pocket. This technique goes well with the classic navy blue, calm gray, and classic tuxedo style suits. Use cotton/linen fabric for this square.

- **Mr. Semi-Conservative:** These folds are similar to "Mr. Conservative" except that they are slightly more pretentious and come to a sharp point. This technique goes well with the bold pinstriped and classic tuxedo style suits. Use cotton/linen fabric for these squares as well.

- **Mr. Blasé:** This fold is actually not a fold at all; it is a puff ... a sexy puff that spills over and appears ostentatious, but is truly the most nonchalant style of all. There is no correct formula to creating this handkerchief. You simply puff it up to your liking and *voila!* You are now sexy without trying! Three dimples in the puff is a nice look if you can pull it off. This technique can be pulled off with the classic navy blue suit, the calm gray, the sexy black suit, the bold pinstriped, and the cool linen/cotton khaki suit. Use linen/silk fabric for this style of handkerchief.

\*\*The more your square/handkerchief is tucked, the less attention you desire. Remember, being Bereolaesque is wearing the hell out of clothes, not letting the clothes wear the hell out of you.

*The Overcoat:* Bold, timeless, and classic, the overcoat is for the gentleman on the go in colder weather. There are several styles and fabrics to choose from; just make sure the cut and fit is close but comfortable. Women love gentlemen in an overcoat!

*The Appeal of a Great Home:* For a gentleman, interior design does not just consist of a television set, porn, and food. A gentleman's place of dwelling is his castle. His home speaks volumes about his life. The personality of a house is indefinable, but should reflect the charm of its owner. Home décor is the gentleman's opportunity to display his style and expose a portion of his soul. Take honor in your home. You don't have to break your bank. There are several ways to shop for less and still have incredible furnishings. Select a color theme for certain areas of the house, to create different moods. Your walls aren't meant to be bare; put some art up. You don't have to go out and get a Picasso or Basquiat (though it would be nice). Find the graphic designer within and manipulate existing digital photos of your own on your laptop. Technology makes it even easier for your work to pass as a modern-day Warhol. Print your work, put it in a frame, and it's as simple as that! Whether you are doing the decorating yourself, or hiring an interior designer, keep in mind that less is always more, but keep it funky.

*I Wear My Sunglasses at Night:* Ray-Bans, aviators, vintage, dark tint, light tint, and faded tint—get them all. Sunglasses not only shield the eyes from dangerous UV rays, but they look good. Indoor or outdoor, it does not matter. Do exercise good judgment when deciding when and where to wear these shades. Excessive access to the eyes is access to the soul; the soul is a very private place ... that's why you wear your sunglasses at night!

**Please do not overdo it with loud colors, obnoxious frames, and pure tackiness— there is an art to wearing sunglasses, and if you lack the pizzazz, you should know right away—give it up.

*iPod:* Music is of immeasurable importance to the Bereolaesque man. A gentleman's music is the entryway to his mind; it is the soundtrack of his life. From the first lullaby sung to our time of departing the earth, music surrounds us. It is part of our relaxation time, our worship, and our holidays. Music accompanies our armies into battle and pays tribute to nations. Dancers find an intimate connection with its melodies, and lovers express emotions through its harmonies. Unlike anything else, music has the ability to reflect, create, and determine our mood, so in essence it says a lot about who were are, what we believe in, and how we feel. Provide channels for music to constantly flow throughout your life. Music is our time machine; it takes us back to a specific place and time with it's first note. Therefore, our musical interests should not be confined to a specific genre. We are eclectic and embrace diversity, remember. Besides, it will make you more well-rounded and relatable. Women find relatable men sexy!

*Toothpick:* Considered tacky in its past life, the toothpick has undergone a public relations makeover. The toothpick is a gentleman's staple. It is a requirement for every Urban Sophisticate. The toothpick is appropriate in all casual environments—*summer soirées, cozy lounges, or hanging with your buddies.* However, this gentleman's piece is unacceptable at any formal, professional, or traditionally religious events.

**Be informed that the toothpick is reserved for the gentleman who is in control of his cool. It is a gentleman's accessory with natural appeal. Do not force the toothpick—do not force the cool.

*Vehicle:* The gentleman's vehicle is an extension of him and should

reflect his personality. However, the Bereolaesque man realizes the importance of priority. We do not invest in a car before we invest in a home!

> *-Must-haves for Every Gentleman's Vehicle:* **change of clothes**—It is important to always, always, always have an extra casual outfit (including a blazer) in your trunk just in case. You never know when you will have an accidental tear, spill, or stain. Remember, adding a blazer to practically any outfit can turn it from casual to sexy. **sugar free gum**—Never know when your mouth will require fresh breath from you. **GPS navigation system/detailed map**—Gentlemen never get lost, right? ... Right. **cell phone**—Obvious reasons. **medicine/first aid kit**—In case of an emergency. **all legal papers**—Have to show something to the right arm of the law when speeding.

*Current Events:* The gentleman is up-to-date on current events (locally and nationwide). He reads his paper (*New York Times*), he watches the news (CNN), or stays updated online (*HuffingtonPost. com*). Being up-to-date on current events is great for knowledge and great for your own well-being—it also comes in handy for conversation starters.

*Subliminally Sexy:* In all that you do, be subtle yet impactful. From the way you dress to the way you speak, the Bereolaesque man is not loud or boastful. He does not intentionally draw attention to himself, though he cannot help but naturally receive it. He makes a T-shirt and jeans stand out tastefully. He is successful but does not show you his bank statement. He is heard without yelling, and makes valid points in few words. He stands out without trying because he realizes that it is not the clothes, possessions, or money that maketh a man; it is the man that maketh the man.

*Walk gently, leaving heavy footprints.*

*Intermission*
*Sight*

*...This Is What it Looks Like ...*

93

# *Interlude*
## *Taste*

# Wine Tasting Etiquette:

## *Remnants of Red & White* [21 to drink]

*-Beautiful body, natural tones, and a taste that makes the lips jealous of the tongue with a trip to ecstasy that justifies the affair ... it may sound like "the other woman" but we're talking wine!*

*To sip a great wine stirs emotion inside you. No matter if you're wearing a suit at a dinner party or underwear at home, a glass of wine makes you feel sexy. It appeals to your five senses, conjures beautiful imagery, and serves as a conversational lubricant. It animates the shy, turns the verbose into the contemplative, and it tastes damn good, too.*

*The best way to get familiar with wine is to attend a wine tasting. Be sure to remain open-minded. There are thousands of wines out there so everyone has his or her own preferences. Here is a concise guide to wine tasting:*

*Eat before you taste. It is not wise to arrive hungry, nor a good idea to rely on food being served. Cheese, crackers, bread, even fruit are often served at wine tastings, but attendees shouldn't expect to do more than nibble.*

*The one exception to this rule is if you are attending a wine dinner/series. Even so, it's more of a tasting menu than full-fledged courses, concentrating more on food-and-wine pairings than hunger management.*

Think sips, not gulps. Organizers of wine tastings typically portion out their wines per attendee, particularly when exclusive or reserve wines are being served. The amount of wine given to each attendee is designed to be a sample; therefore, the glass will not be full.

You aren't there to get drunk, so no asking for seconds unless the organizers offer. Skipping one wine in a series does not give you a free pass for double of something else that you think you will enjoy more. Buy a bottle and savor it at home.

Get on intimate terms with your wine. Even a beginner can understand the rudiments of the wine experience. The first thing you should do is look at the wine in the glass. Pick up the glass by the stem, not the bowl. You do not want crappy fingerprints to cloud your view; wine is sexy ... so enjoy its splendor. It is also the belief that the temperature of your hand may compromise the temperature of the wine you're about to taste—red wine excluded. Hold the wine up to the light and look at its color and clarity. Then explore the bouquet of the wine.

The next step is to take a sip. You want to bring a little air into your mouth as you take a sip, to help release the flavors in your mouth.

The process requires you to taste the wine in the front and back of your mouth. The back of your mouth will pick up the tannins in the wine; it will also help you release it's esters into your sinuses.

Beginners can easily pick up floral or fruit notes; the more experienced are likely to cue in on more sophisticated nuances. Each individual person will pick up different things in a wine. It's a subjective process and there is no right or wrong response.

Spitting is socially acceptable. Though polite American society regards spitting as a serious social faux pas, the spittoon (or dump bucket) is alive, well, and acceptable at a wine tasting. After you have finished tasting each wine, it is appropriate to pour out the remaining wine in your glass. I, however, if enjoying the taste—prefer to enjoy it all.

If spittoons or buckets are not within reach, you can simply leave the wine in a glass or designate an empty glass as a community dump—just do not accidentally sample it!

True spitting also is allowed and can be done with grace. The more alcohol you consume, the less likely you will truly taste the later wine samples.

It is an educational experience, not a cocktail party. Though a wine tasting is indeed a social activity, common courtesy should still prevail. You and your companions should not talk over the organizers or guest cellar master or other wine representative.

Wine tastings often follow a rhythm that begins with the introduction of each wine. This can range from a "quick spiel" to complex information if a representative from the winery is present. The experience level of guests usually ranges from novices to experts, so don't be afraid to ask questions.

*Beginners should not feel intimidated. If you are uncomfortable at a wine tasting, do not go back. There are plenty of other places in the area where the people are down-to-earth and willing to share a positive wine experience with you.*

*The more wine tastings you attend, the more types of wines, vintages, regions, and vintners you will experience. Over time, you will more expertly understand and enjoy the whole wine experience. You may want to create a wine journal. Pick it up from Crate and Barrel—Beverly Hills. Bring it with you to the tasting, documenting and analyzing each taste in the journal or upon returning home. Describe your emotions and write your own reviews. Either way, a wine journal will be useful and enjoyable to refer back to in the months and years ahead!*

**Cabernet**—Associated with cherry, olive, or plum

**Chardonnay**—Tastes like apple, lemon, or melon

**Pinot Noir**—Similar to zinfandel, with earthiness, peppercorn, and lavender

**Riesling**—Compared to grapefruit, jasmine, and cinnamon

**Zinfandel**—Generally associated with blackberry, pomegranate, and wood

**Favorable Wine Serving Temperatures:**

**White Wines:** 45-50° F or 7-10° C

**Red Wines:** 50-65° F or 10-18° C

**Rosé Wines:** 45-55° F or 7-13° C

**Sparkling Wines:** 42-52° F or 6-11° C

**Fortified Wines:** 55-68° F or 13-20° C

**-Drink Responsibly**

# The Temple

# The Temple: *A Gentleman's Frame*

A gentleman's frame is what sex is to a healthy married relationship—*essential*. Each gentleman recognizes his body as his temple and respects it as such. He does not consume too many fatty foods or an excess of libations damaging to the liver.

He is completely conscious of his healthy being as well as he is the food that he eats. Lean meats are preferable to other meat. And a daily glass of red wine is preferable to a daily glass of scotch.

Conscious eating and routine exercising is for the disciplined gentleman. It is something that takes adjusting to. Rid your refrigerator of the junky, fatty foods and replace them with healthy contents: fruit, vegetables, fish, lean meats, etc.

Below are several options of healthy meals for the day.
*Sexy Food Items*

BREAKFAST
English muffin, bacon egg/spinach omelet, and fruit

Or

Whole-grain cereal topped with fruit and cottage cheese or yogurt

SNACK

Protein shake (1 orange, 1 apple, 1 ounce almonds, 1 cup fat-free
vanilla yogurt, 1 scoop vanilla whey protein powder)

Or

Power shake (1 banana, 1 tablespoon flax oil, 1 cup green tea)

Or

Apple, green tea

Walnuts

LUNCH

Tuna sandwich (mayonnaise, relish, pickles, and tomatoes)

Grilled chicken salad

Or

Grilled chicken

SNACK

Sugar-free Jell-O and/or sugar-free pudding

Or

2 apples, walnuts, carrots

DINNER

Salmon or tilapia

Potato

2 cups spinach

Or

Lean red meat, brown rice, mixed veggies

Or

Spaghetti


Eating healthily is not the only formula for keeping the temple cleansed—exercise is the other half of the agreement. Coupling exercise with a healthy diet results in a sexy outcome. It will not only have you looking good, but it will also have you feeling good. When you look good and you feel good, you will behave well. When you behave well, you are Bereolaesque!

# A Gentleman's Guide to Healthy Eating

There are many reasons that all of us should eat healthily. A few reasons why health is important is that it helps with body processes, promotes the growth and repairing of cells, and it provides energy. Eating healthily also reduces risks of diseases such as cancer, coronary heart disease, stroke, diabetes, and osteoporosis. Fatty foods and excessive drinking plant the seeds for these health issues. Everything in moderation is essential to a healthy lifestyle. A healthy diet also helps you maintain a desirable weight and body frame. A great tool that one can follow to promote healthy eating and a balanced diet, is following the guidelines of the Food Pyramid.

Calorie intake is also a big consideration! Men should take in at least 2,000 to 2,500 calories a day. Women need at least 1,500 to 2,000 calories a day. For more active men and women, those numbers are likely to increase.

One of the biggest mistakes people make when trying to lose weight is skipping meals. Did you know that your metabolism slows down about fifty percent closer to midnight? Therefore, eating habits that end before the late evening are digested faster and processed by the body for maximum nutrient intake.

Our body is like an automobile in a way—in the morning it expects nourishment that acts as fuel to get the metabolism going. If your first meal is around noon, your first good calorie is burned shortly thereafter. I say *good calorie* because when your body is not fed, it hangs on to calories and fat to survive! The body refuses to starve, so you gain more weight skipping breakfast and other meals.

Another issue is eating habits. I figure some people don't eat breakfast because they tend to think it needs to be a large serving … not the case. None of your meals needs to be large at all. Be satisfied when finishing a meal, not stuffed. Have a piece of toast or fruit, and milk or juice to get your day started and your metabolism going. Give yourself up to two weeks to start feeling the energy and liveliness. When practicing this lifestyle, you will notice you aggressively become hungrier—this is a positive thing. This process means your body is burning fat and requires more quality food!

There are a lot of interesting facts and science to feeling your best and learning about your body. If you think you're sexy on the outside, wait until you start from within. Mind, body, and spirit are what make the flesh. Find out how great you can feel!

*Some healthy recipes that are easy to make:*

**Couscous Salad:** *serves 4 – 8*

*Big bowl needed.*

*-1 3/4 cups couscous*

*-1/4 cup dried apples*

*-1/4 cup dried cranberries*

*-1/4 cup dried apricots*

*- 1/2 bunch fresh mint (chopped)*

*- 1/4 cup roasted pine nuts*

*- 1/3 cup olive oil*

*- 1 lemon, juice and zest*

*- sprinkle of salt/pepper*

*Directions:*

*Place couscous in a large bowl and pour over 2 cups of boiling water. Cover and set aside for five to ten minutes, then fluff with a fork (prepare ingredients in the mean time). Add remaining ingredients—season with salt and pepper. Mix well and enjoy!*

*\* You can enjoy this salad for lunch, dinner, or a snack.*

**Yogurt Parfait:** *Serves 2*

- 12 ounces yogurt (pick a flavor)

- ½ cup granola cereal

- ½ cup sliced banana

½ cup fresh blueberries

Directions:

In glass cups, layer yogurt, granola, and fruit.

\* *This is a light and healthy breakfast.*

**Balsamic Portobello & Mozzarella**

**Ciabatta:** Serves 2

- 1 large Portobello mushroom

- 1 fresh ball of mozzarella cheese

- 1 small red onion

- ½ cup fresh spinach

- 2 loafs of ciabatta bread

- 2 tablespoons pesto sauce

- 2 teaspoons balsamic vinegar

Directions:

Marinate Portobello mushroom in balsamic
vinegar. Grill mushroom and slice evenly.
Sauté red onions until translucent. Toast
ciabatta bread. Add Portobello mushroom,

*sliced mozzarella, warm red onions, fresh*

*spinach and spread pesto sauce on bread.*

\* <u>*Great sandwich for lunch or dinner!*</u>

*-Enjoy.*


**—Everett E. Frampton,** *personal chef/health consultant*

The ?uestion

# The ?uestion: *Elegance under Pressure*
## *Keeping It Cool, Calm, Collected*

In order to consider our next subject, we offer two separate definitions of the word "elegant." Here is the Bereolaesque understanding of the term:

Elegant: demonstrating style and sophistication in appearance and behavior.

We are going to merge this idea with the mathematical definition:

Elegant: combining simplicity, authority, and superior design.

"Elegance" in science or math refers to a concept so powerful and elementary that it almost defies description—the concept may have even been overlooked due to its simplicity. In our world of social interaction, we strive for this fundamental quality of behavior—manners so ingrained that they become seamless, superior, and simple. If this is the case, then our goal must be not just to embrace excellent manners as our mission but also to apply those manners in every situation and circumstance. In short, excellent manners do us no good if we throw them away under stress.

Being a gentleman is not something that one turns on and off. It is not a mere act that one displays in order to achieve some sort of credibility, recognition, or a pat on the almighty back. Being a gentleman is simply being you to the very best of your ability every day that God allows you to breathe—and if you fall short, simply pick up this book and flip to this chapter. We all need to be reminded every once in a while. For goodness' sake, nobody is perfect ... but we can all afford to be a little more Bereolaesque!

*To err is human, but to err without correction is failure.* In the quest to being Bereolaesque, there are several situations where one is left in the dark, not knowing what to do, where to go, and how to ask. Allow me to enlighten you. I have come up with three basic principles:

1. **Keeping It Cool**—In order to "keep it cool," we have to dissect each event of action taking place.

2. **Maintaining Manners**—This rule of thumb will allow you to live life with less stress and more smiles.

3. **Being Bereolaesque (use book as reference)**—Why wouldn't you refer to this book? It has all the answers ...

We have all been in uncomfortable or stressful scenarios. Oftentimes, what makes an experience uncomfortable is our lack of knowledge of how to approach it or our fears of being judged. What makes a situation stressful is our reaction to it, so in essence we create our own stress. Well, let us throw all of that crap out of the window and address these uncomfortable or stressful scenarios head-on. Below are several generic examples of potentially uncomfortable situations. Though the scenarios differ, applying the three basic principle concepts of keeping it cool, maintaining manners, and being Bereolaesque will make for a positive outcome in each scene.

### Scenario 1: *Forgetting somebody's name or an important date:*

We are Bereolaesque gentlemen; we are constantly meeting different people with different names, and oftentimes we get busy. Let's face it, we forget names from time to time. Names are important, but do not make a huge deal of forgetting one or two. If you have already been introduced to someone and you forget their name, kindly ask them to repeat it; simple as that. You can lighten the mood by saying, "I am sorry, I have the worst memory; tell me your name one more time." If you are just too embarrassed to ask, there are a few clever ways that I have come up with to find out: 1. **Business Scenario:** *Ask him or her for a business card.* All contact information will be on the card. **Casual Scenario:** *Have him or her put his or her information in your phone.* This will include the person's name. 2. **Business Scenario:** *Ask what he or she prefers to be called.* Generally in business environments, people give their full names. Using this method will not only force them to repeat their name, but it will show that you respect their preference. **Casual Scenario:** *Ask him or her to spell it.* If it is a unique name, it is acceptable to compliment the person and kindly ask how it is spelled or if it has any significance. 3. *Ask a mutual party.* In most cases, you were introduced to the person whose name you forgot by a mutual party. Find a moment to ask your party to discreetly repeat the guest's name. Try breaking the habit of forgetting names. If you can remember your own name, remember someone else's. Just keep it cool and maintain your manners!

## Scenario 2: *Declining an invitation:*

It is gentlemanly to accept an invitation. However, we cannot be in five places at one time. Simply let them know you have a prior engagement and thank them for the offer. A social gentleman does not decline more than five invitations at any given time.

**Scenario 3:** *Someone you met calls you by the wrong name:*

It is okay to let it slide the first time around. If it happens again, do not hesitate to correct them kindly.

**Scenario 4:** *Being introduced to your significant other's parents:*

Greet them with a warm smile, acknowledging the father first and the mother second. Remember to shake the father's hand with a firm web-to-web handshake. Consider the rule: If you are under thirty, you may refer to him as sir and the mother as madam (ma'am) until told otherwise. If you are over thirty, it is appropriate to refer to them by Mr. and Mrs. followed by their last name. If the mother is traditional, she may present her

hand and motion it downward; this is a sign for you to kiss it.
Take a slight bow and reach for her hand, lightly kissing it. Do
not be obnoxious and make a scene. If she is more relaxed, you
may greet the mother with a subtle handshake, a slight hug, or
a kiss on the cheek. It is up to you to make the quick judgment
call. Remember to keep it cool and maintain your manners;
they are probably just as nervous as you are. A genuine
compliment wouldn't hurt in this scenario.

**Scenario 5:** *Placing someone on hold:*
Phone conversations can be intense, important, and many
other adjectives that fill this page. Whether it is for business,
pleasure, or a little bit of both, being Bereolaesque will probably
have your phone ringing quite often. Old phone etiquette says
that you should engage in one phone call at a time; this form
of etiquette is outdated. It is acceptable to place a call on hold
for a brief period. Hold time should not exceed ten to twenty
seconds. If you know the person on the other line will exceed
that time, let it go to voicemail and return their call promptly.
Maintain manners when placing the call on hold. Words like
*excuse me* and *please* are fitting for situations such as this one.
Refrain from placing any important calls on hold.

**Scenario 6:** *Any form of awkward silence:*

These moments are sometimes unavoidable. They come out of nowhere and often leave all parties involved feeling uncomfortable. Although you do not have complete control over silent moments, you do have control over how long they last. Use the silent moment to think of something to fill it with. Asking general (not personal) questions is a great way to get the other person talking. Easy conversation starters are current events. Avoid controversial conversation—*politics*—as you do not want to offend anybody. Neutral topics like sports are also easy subjects to call to attention. You can even talk about the past ten minutes of your life if anything interesting happened. Being generally observant and in tune with people can be of benefit when controlling awkward silence. Notice what the person is wearing, who they are with, topics they may bring up, and how they behave—these are all great gauges of what someone's interests are. Anticipating moments of silence will help you think of great ways to cover them up.

**Scenario 7:** *Being in the presence of an unfamiliar person who passes gas:*

Let us not act like we have never passed gas. Hold in your laugh and try your best not to react; it would only further embarrass the perpetrator. If the person has any decency, he or she will say *excuse me* and let it be.

**Scenario 8:** *Excusing yourself from a talkative person:*

This can be quite the arduous task, but no need to fret. Simply excuse yourself and provide a valid reason. Emergencies, the kids, or a prior engagement will all suffice. You can even secretly call someone and hang up—they'll be sure to call you right back. When they do call back, let the talkative person know that it is an important call.

**Scenario 9:** *You are mutual friends with a couple and realize that one of them is cheating:*

Advise each friend that you are aware of the situation and suggest they confront it. That's it! Don't get yourself caught in the middle. It is not up to you to be the solution to all of life's problems—merely an advocate of what is correct!

**Scenario 10:** *Being in the presence of an ex:*

Always play it casual—don't bring unnecessary attention to the scene. Be cordial and leave it at that. No sense in making a potentially awkward situation worse.

**Scenario 11:** *Tripping over something or falling on the ground:*

You're Bereolaesque … who cares! Gather yourself, recover, and quickly move on—no need to dwell on the situation. Pick your face off the ground and play it cool. Drawing attention to the scenario will only make matters worse.

**Scenario 12:** *Spilling a drink:*

Quickly apologize, clean it up, and offer to buy another one— you see, this is simple stuff—remember, common sense plays an integral role in being Bereolaesque.

**Scenario 13:** *Running out of money at a restaurant:*

This should never happen, but if your date happens to give you a run for your money … erase her number! No, really, if this does happen to you, use your credit card, but you should always carry enough cash to pay for two dinners. A gentleman should have a credit card and emergency cash on him at all times.

**Scenario 14:** *Dealing with rude people:*

These types of people have a way of getting under your skin, no matter how nice of a guy you are. What I find always works is a smile. It does not matter how tough you are or how weird this may sound … it works. Kindness kills rudeness! Never react negatively. That does not mean you should be weak and fail to stand your ground. Make your point assertively but in a pleasant manner—keep it gentlemanly—keep it Bereolaesque.

**Scenario 15:** *Asking a favor of a stranger:*

We have all been in cars that are too cold, homes that are too hot, or in the presence of radios that are just too loud. Not everyone will ask your opinion, offer you a cold drink, or ask you if their music's pitch is to your liking. Usually there is a third party or mutual friend you depend on as your liaison, but sometimes we are left in these uncomfortable situations to fend for ourselves. What to do? Simple … maintain your manners and kindly say "excuse me" and present your request. Most of the time, our minds are making the situation much bigger than it is anyway. When you request something, there will always be a 50 percent chance of hearing a *yes* and a 50 percent chance of hearing *no*. When you choose not to ask at all, there is a 100 percent chance of hearing *no*; closed mouths do not get fed. Is it really that difficult to ask someone for a ride? Do not allow pride, fear, or discomfort to dictate your situation. You are in control of your life … the only person that stands in your way is you!

**Scenario 16:** *Realizing that you and a friend are dating the same girl:*

Happens all the time, right? In all seriousness, this situation will most likely occur at some point in your lifetime. Whether she is a current or a past dealing, friends dating friends' friends is probable among any group. A scenario like this is not one to lose a best bud over. See how your buddy truly feels about the ideal of you courting the same—*or previous*—lady that he hangs (hung) with. Make sure to ask when the two of you are by yourselves—men have the tendency to act macho, as if important matters don't bother them in the presence of other men. If it disturbs him, he isn't fit to be Bereolaesque! In all seriousness, a scenario like this is left upon the discretion of the parties involved. The two most important factors to consider are not to let the situation affect the relationship of you and your buddy and not to let it affect the relationship of you and your lady friend. Avoid quarrels and catfights; it doesn't look good on you!

*Professional Gentleman of Leisure*

# *The Professional Gentleman of Leisure:*
## *Meeting People Who Meet People*

## Succeed with Style

- Socialites

- Events

- Travel

## Socialites

People enjoy people who enjoy what they enjoy. We have the tendency to think that social arts are more complicated than they actually are. We get nervous about holding a meaningful five-minute face-to-face conversation with someone new, but we are comfortable having never-ending meaningless conversations online. A socialite simply enjoys the social life. The only thing separating a stranger from an associate is a *hello*. After the hello, that associate will find him- or herself wanting to associate with you.

Work the room without being too involved. Don't be the first to arrive or the last to leave. A simple rule of thumb about meeting folks on the social scene (networking) is to be yourself—*considering you've already read this book cover to cover.*

One of the most fundamental rules of life is that perception is reality. With that being said, it is important that the way you are perceived is indeed in line with reality.

First impressions are fundamental in being Bereolaesque. Before stepping on the scene, make sure you are always presentable. Don't go out disgracing yourself *(refer to Style Blueprint)*. Keeping it Bereolaesque means allowing others entryway into your sexy. When meeting people, allow them to see your *certain something*—that thing that separates you from the rest. I'm not suggesting that you put on or show off for others, but do let your natural charisma pour from your pores. In other words, let others see you at your best when they see you first.

When you greet someone or are in a conversation, certainly use their name within dialogue. It displays a sense of familiarity and a sense of trust. Do not forget to place the appropriate title in front of a name when necessary.

**Connect with people.** On the social and professional scenes, we meet people daily and forget about them within the hour. Connecting with people is the key to unlocking the networking door. A gentleman is able to uphold a decent conversation without cease or lack of interest.

He pleasantly engages without rambling, and is keen on making lasting impressions quickly. Being contemporary allows for great conversation and noteworthy dialogue.

People enjoy people who enjoy what they enjoy—it is the basis of how friendships are started. Study the person before you are introduced to them. Notice what they are wearing, saying, how they move, and what they are doing. It is even okay to inquire about them to a mutual friend. Find out their interests and how you relate. After beginning dialogue, find a smooth way to incorporate their interests into your conversation. There is chemistry to natural dialogue. Never be forceful, and always be you.

Mixing It Up

A Bereolaesque man is one who adjusts equally well to finer as well as plainer society. He is able to adapt in any setting and maintain his charisma as well as his relatability. The more subjects he knows about, the more people he is in common with, and therefore the more clients, associates, or constituents he is sure to have. Social etiquette must include ethics as well as manners. A gentleman's manners are an integral part of him and are the same whether in his bedroom or in a ballroom, whether addressing a CEO or a janitor.

# Events

When a gentleman is entertaining, his only two goals are to enjoy his company and make sure they enjoy him. He is not out to make impressions. Now is not the time to put on your top hat and begin your tap routine. Events are truly a gentleman's time to relax and enjoy the festivities.

Mix and mingle in the crowd, but don't be overzealous. As long as you are Bereolaesque, you will be noticed without having to be noticed. Be cordial to people you don't know and genuinely pleased to see those you do. If someone catches your eye, do not be afraid to approach her—*you remember what we've learned thus far.*

Let your confidence shine through your garments, but do keep it under control. Don't allow your confidence to overwhelm your humility and turn to narcissism. You probably received several compliments on your outfit, but get a hold of yourself. The gentleman who can take a compliment with a smile and move on is the gentleman people want to be around.

Whether courtside, outside, or by her side, always keep it Bereolaesque!

## Travel—The Jet Fuel Abuser

Traveling is what the gentleman does. He is immune to jet lag, and has more places to be and less time to get there. He not only conducts business out of town, but he is the international man.

- **Pack smart**
- **Dress comfortably**
- **Carry your female companion's luggage**
- **Put your shades on**
- **Relax**
- **Keep it Bereolaesque**

**Packing Smart**: When a journey entails long hours, be sure to pack accordingly. Invest in quality items that don't wrinkle easily when folded. Nothing is worse than finally arriving at your destination having to worry about ironing.

**Dressing Comfortably**: What you wear on a flight is as important as the flight itself. Turbulence, unfriendly passengers, and bad food can make for a bad mile-high experience. Don't add the equation by wearing some stiff suit for lengthy hours. The Urban Sophisticate invests in unlined blazers that fit comfortably while giving off a distinct appeal. Cashmere is an excellent thread for comfort.

**Carry Your Female Companion's Luggage**: Unless it is simple to maneuver, a female companion should never carry her own luggage. Whether you or the skycap does the honors, make sure your guest never struggles with her trunks or bags—you are a gentleman, get to work!

**Put Your Shades On**: The airport can be a stressful world of delays, overbooked seats, and undisciplined children. Sunglasses can remove you from a world of chaos and place you into your very own comfort zone. Regardless of the time of day, put your shades on—it allows you to escape from the madness while keeping your cool!

**Relax**: Whether the getaway is business or pleasure—*or both*—anticipating the arrival can cause unnecessary stress and anxiety. Plan out your trip in advance to avoid the sweat. Bring your iPod, a newspaper, some work, or a great contemporary gentleman and etiquette book to read! You'll get to your destination, sir. Sit back, relax, and enjoy the different characters walking through the airport.

**Keep It Bereolaesque**: It is the common theme throughout this book. It shouldn't be difficult to do, right?

*You Don't Have Enough Stamps on Your Passport*—If you are planning on going Bereolaesque, plan on going international. Be sure to school yourself on the no-nos of the culture you are heading to. Practicing general etiquette in human interaction is okay, but this brief list will help you avoid embarrassment, disrespect, and even death altogether, by doing your homework.

*Research:* Examine the culture of the country. Find out what is acceptable and what is not. Ask someone from the culture about the social mores and cultural customs. There is plenty of information available online as well.

*Know the Language:* Get familiar with the language of the county you are visiting. Study the fundamentals of the language so that you are able to do the following: *locate a restroom, inquire about food, get directions, and tell a woman she is beautiful!*—do research the customs of the country before complimenting a woman. There are countries where a foreign visitor could be jailed or even sentenced to death for doing this.

*Practice:* As crazy as this may sound, rehearsing customs develops your familiarity with the culture and will make your interaction more natural—not forced.

*Politics:* Is the country in the middle of a war? Are elections coming up? Knowing when to visit another country can mean the difference between life and death.

## Netiquette—The Cyber Life

The internet can be an interesting place—so interesting, that you lose focus and toss all you've learned about etiquette out the window. Let's not do that! The world wide web serves the greater purpose of keeping people connected among other things. This connection requires the same, if not more, etiquette than the *real world*.

When entering cyberspace, we tend to forget that we are still in a community dealing with real people. We fail to see facial expressions, hear tones, or study gestures so we make all sorts of mistakes, relying on the anonymity of a screen name to protect us. We feel a sense of power behind that protection … so much so that we often say and do things we would never do in *real life*.

Now I'm not indicating an occasional escape from reality isn't well deserved at times, but do keep it all in perspective gentlemen. It's sometimes difficult to effectively communicate online, making it quite easy to misinterpret information. Keep this in mind when engaging in dialog. Exercise the same etiquette you would in reality as you do on the internet. This goes for text messaging as well as all forms of electronic communication.

-No stalking!

*Interlude*
*Smell*

# Cigar Etiquette: *Cumulus Clouds/Liquid Smoke*

*\*\*Do not use tobacco if you are under the age of eighteen or have serious health problems.*

**The Bereolaesque gentleman indulges in the occasional cigar, mainly during celebratory events (infrequently). Social activities are acceptable as well, but let us not make it a habit—tobacco smoke increases the risk of lung cancer and heart disease.**

Dating back long ago, the cigar is a gentleman's delicacy. Intimidating in its appearance, enjoying the cigar may seem to be quite the arduous task. Premium/luxury cigars are handmade by experts from perfectly aged top-quality blends of tobacco, and can be quite costly. Relax! Do not let these facts scare you. Here is a guide to getting lost in these cumulus clouds:

*The Selection:* Choosing the perfect cigar is entirely up to you. However, there are some key elements to look for. The leaf that the tobacco is wrapped in, the filler, and the binder give each cigar its distinct taste.

  • **The Maduro** leaf is dark brown in color, due to its natural exposure to sunlight. This exposure extracts the sugar from the leaf, leaving a sweet taste. If you like your cigars rich, full, and sweet, this slowly burning Maduro is for you.

- **The Natural** leaf is brown in color and is hung to dry. It provides a slightly sweet taste and slower burn, due to its natural oil content.
- **The Claro** leaf is green or light brown in color because it is shielded from sunlight. This leaves the leaf with little sugar/oil content, causing a quicker burn and a practically mild cigar.

Due to a vast array of options, selecting the perfect cigar is like selecting the perfect car. Don't hesitate to ask your local tobacconist for assistance. The size of the cigar depends on your preference. Generally, the larger the cigar, the longer the burn time will be. Shorter cigars are proportioned differently, which can influence the taste.

*The Cut:* Cigars taste and smoke differently, depending upon how they are clipped. One should clip the cigar with a quality cutter at the head (closed end) of the cigar closest to the cap (identifiable by a distinct line near the head). To avoid drying out, do not clip the cigar until the moment you are ready to indulge—store the cigar in a humidor until ready for use. When using a bullet-punch cutter, just insert the punch on the head of the cigar to cut a small hole.

*The Fire:* The lighting process is a fiery romantic affair between you and your cigar. Apply the flame from your custom lighter under the cigar, rotating it for a thorough burn. Remove any ash the fire creates. Enjoy the aroma it provokes.

*The Affair*: Smoking a fine cigar is like an intimate moment with the one you love, so take your time. Hold the cigar between your index finger and thumb. Take long draws and hold the smoke in without inhaling it. Release the smoke but refrain from being obnoxious about it, as it is not in line with proper etiquette.

Liquid Smoke—Enjoying a drink with your cigar is like sex. Pairing the right cigar with the right drink is the orgasm. Certain drinks bring out flavors and overtones in cigars that otherwise go unnoticed. Here is a guideline to the indulgence:

# Liquid Smoke

| Intoxicating | Non-Alcoholic |
|---|---|
| ***Scotch on the rocks*** | ***Coffee/Espressos*** |
| Pulls flavor from any cigar | Complements the natural cigar |

***Rum*** (Good quality, of course)

Perfect complement to any great cigar

***Cognac*** (VSOP/XO)

Goes well after meals with the natural cigar

***Vodka***

Goes perfectly with any Davidoff cigar

Series rich aroma and smooth taste

***Kahlua***

This style of drink is the perfect fit for Maduro cigars

***Fruity martinis***

Men DO NOT drink them, therefore do not
smoke with them

**Red Wine**

Companion to a fine cigar of any type

**Drafts**

Pair a natural cigar with your booze

*\*\*Do not consume alcoholic beverages if you*
*are under the age of twenty-one.*

*The Farewell*: All is well that ends well, and good things must come to an end. It is poor etiquette to "butt out" a cigar, as it will create an unpleasant odor for everyone around you. Allow it to die out on its own. If you are not prepared to finish the cigar, do not light it—store it in a humidor and let it breathe.

# The Affair

# The Affair: *Social Intercourse*
## *Dating*

While single, being Bereolaesque makes you an extremely eligible bachelor. While dating, being Bereolaesque keeps her running back for more. When married, being Bereolaesque qualifies you as the world's greatest husband. You are among an elite ranking of few. But it all starts with the approach.

Contrary to popular belief, there truly are several ways to approach a lady. The approach may vary depending on your personality and the scenario. The two things that are crucial are confidence and gaining a good understanding of the woman you are approaching and women in general.

### TREAT HER LIKE A LADY

Each woman is different, so don't be foolish enough to believe that the same style that impressed the last will impress the next. Different women have different preferences, so watch—*not stalk*—her from a distance and pay attention to her vibe before any advancement is considered. Knowing what a woman wants beforehand and being able to provide is key.

## Artistic Flirtation

Flirting is indeed an art. It involves intense movement of the eyes, the words one allows to flow from his or her mouth, the tone/pitch/speed of voice, the movement and demeanor of the body, the unobservable energy flowing through a room from you to her, and a welcomed invasion of personal space.

Flirting merely displays the intensity of a connection between two people. Gentlemen are masters of the art. We pick up on people's vibes and know when to take flirting to the next level and when to stop.

Flirting doesn't require a sexual tone; it is a friendly person's sport. Those who are receptive to it find you to be fun-loving and pleasant to be around. Flirts are no strangers to perks—free upgrades, free tickets, discounts, pardons, etc. We often find ourselves in others' good graces because of our genuinely kind nature.

Be cautious! Acceptable flirting varies from person to person. Overstepping the boundaries is among the most serious faux pas one can commit. Flirting has no place in the corporate arena—a gentleman avoids lawsuits at all costs. There is a time and a place for everything. Refrain from flirting with a married woman, even if she is flirtatious with you.

FIRST

## Have Her at Hello

Sometimes all you have to do is say hi! It is not always as difficult as us men make it out to be. Forget the flashy clothes, the corny pick-up line, and the preparatory speech; just say hello. Women sense sincerity and embrace genuineness; being real is sexy. A simple hello can truly spark quality conversation and garner interest. But watch out for placement in the "friend zone." Gentlemen who know what they are doing do not end up there.

## THE CASUAL APPROACH

Close your eyes with me for a moment and imagine this: You are at the bookstore, intently studying the pages of *Bereolaesque*. You briefly lift your head and notice a strikingly attractive woman picking up a copy of *Bereolaesque* as well. From her uncanny beauty and your obvious mutual interests in literature, you find yourself interested to know more about this nameless lady. You decide that you are going to approach her! Wait ... not yet. Engage in a friendly game of flirting first. Never seem overeager. Women appreciate an assertive yet patient and mysterious gentleman. Catch frequent eye contact and smile. Do not stare at her ... well, unless she is just that beautiful! If you are as Bereolaesque as you think you are, she is probably attracted to you too, but she probably will not approach you. Though women are becoming more aggressive with time, as gentlemen we generally have to initiate the approach. Think of this moment as a once-in-a-lifetime opportunity and you may never run into this mystery lady again. If she kindly entertains your flirtatious efforts, confidently approach her and introduce yourself.

**Pro**: Many women enjoy the thrill of a confident mystery man.

**Con**: If you're too much of a mystery, she may become an unsolved mystery. Sometimes a woman may be interested, but will show no signs. You have to utilize keen discernment.

## THE AGGRESSIVE APPROACH

Hey, some women like it rough! Women who are typically on the shy side like for a man to be a man. Often these polar opposites have an uncanny attraction for one another.

**Pro**: You may get what you're looking for.

**Con**: This approach may leave you with hand marks across your face … unless she is just into that type of stuff.

## THE NONCHALANT APPROACH

This approach requires little to no work at all. You just stand back and let your charming energy create attention for itself. If you are Mr. Cool himself, this approach just may work. Generally if a woman finds you attractive, she will know within the first three seconds of seeing you. If this is the case, she will react. It may be blatant or subtle, and if you are good, you can catch this reaction. To know whether you are on the right track, look for signals the other person is sending through body language, such as pupil dilation, blushing, leaning closer, more hand contact, and shared focus—simply glancing at her may be enough to get her attention. Keep in mind this is for the gentleman who has mastered the art of being Bereolaesque.

**Pro**: Women are attracted to sexy and drawn to cool. You may notice you've prompted the interest of more than a few.

**Con**: If not naturally executed to perfection, this approach can turn a woman off and leave Mr. Cool all by his cool self. Don't force the cool— if you've got it, then you've got it.

# THE BEREOLAESQUE APPROACH:

You tell her that you are positive that fate allowed for this opportune moment and you are certain that the two of you would have an incredible time together. You tell her that you have set aside an entire day exclusively tailored for her—ask when she is free …

**Pro**: This approach is genuine and can be played by you as simply platonic or incredibly romantic. The two of you have an amazing time together. She is able to see how creative and/or romantic you are, depending on what you decide to do. She is able to capture the essence of who you are and what you stand for. She recognizes the extreme measures you've taken to ensure that she has a fun, relaxing, and thought-provoking encounter. She is intrigued and her interest (whether romantic or not) in you has peaked.

**Con**: You might have a stalker … I'm kidding! This approach may be considered over the top and more appropriate for a second or third date. A woman with her defenses up due to an unfamiliar environment and an unpredictable companion is not the best path to courtship and getting closer. Do not scare the girl away on the first date. Be sure to exercise good judgment—her level of comfort should be your main concern.

**Approaching a Woman When She Is with a Group of Friends**

Be very confident and be neutral in this approach. Try not to approach the one that you are interested in first. Approach her friend—the one who guys usually do not approach—because she has the most say-so in the group. Spark a general conversation that is interesting enough for everyone to engage in or that requires an answer from each member of the group. Eventually the woman you are interested in will let down her guard when she realizes you are not there just to pick up on her and she will become involved in the conversation. The rest is up to you … keeping it Bereolaesque should result in a date minus the friends.

Each approach offers the potential for more, or a pathway for her to walk out the door. Think about your options and choose what feels right to you. If you are naturally laid back and would feel incredibly out of place in a fancy restaurant, pick your favorite lounge; if she hates local lounges, then you are not meant to be—kidding. Or if you are more into making a stylish first impression, go someplace where you can show her your originality.

NEXT

# Giving Her the Business ... Card

After the approach, kindly offer to exchange contact information. But do not pull out your bulky PDA. If you really want to gauge a lady's interest, slide her your business card, kindly ask for hers, and part ways. It's a bit impersonal, but this is a good way to determine if a woman is truly interested in you. If she calls you on a personal level based off of your business card, she's interested! This neutral approach saves you the embarrassment of being denied her phone number, and at the same time allows you to present yours without feeling awkward or too aggressive. If you just can't bank on her calling, give her a ring ... not an engagement ring, a phone call. If the conversation goes well, ask her if she would like to continue in person or over dinner.

THEN

# First Date

First dates are a piece of cake but can be trouble if you allow it. There is really no getting around the fact that two new people coming together for the sole purpose of getting to know one another can be a delicate awkwardness. But the first step toward a better first date is recognizing this challenge.

Dating is what it is—two strangers trying to decide if they ever want to see each other again. Once you have made your peace with this fact and found some comfort in the unknown, you have made some excellent progress.

It does no one any good to panic. No need to apply layer after layer of cologne or go brushing and re-brushing your teeth until you are bleeding at the gums. Instead think about the fact that the other person is probably just as nervous as you are—and that no matter what, there will be the potential for an enjoyable moment.

Of course, once you have stopped panicking, the next step is to revisit your approach. There is a spectrum of casual versus formal behavior that is at play here, and it can work for you or against you. How did you ask her out? Did you ask her to "go out" or to "hook up"? Where are you taking her? And are you picking her up or are you meeting there? By the way, a gentleman always offers to pick up ... it can be of benefit later.

## Second Date

If you have made it past your first date, you should be relieved. The most uncertain phase is over and the detective work begins for real. Think about how the first date went. Was there a lot of warm flirting or lusty glances and arm touching? Or did she spend a lot of time avoiding eye contact, visiting and revisiting the restroom, and/or studying the keypad of her BlackBerry?

Did you find lots in common to talk about? Or were you struggling to fill the silence and praying your waiter would come over and make small talk about the bread? Did she leave you with the impression that she wanted to see you again or is it a wrap?

If you think the date went well enough that you have a chance at a second date, wait a full forty-eight hours and then call her. If you call her immediately, she might take it as a sign that you're desperate (and you may be). If the two of you were obviously vibing, go on and give her a call or send a text message, letting her know how great of a time you had a few hours after the date.

Use this second-date phone call to continue your detective work. Does she sound happy to hear from you? Does she sound completely apathetic or does she start going on and on about what a great time she had too? If you get her voicemail, leave her a message but do not ask her out in the actual message. That would leave her with a lot of time to perfectly craft a response, which will make your phone call less useful for investigative purposes.

If she is willing to go out with you again, now is the time to really get to know each other as human beings and not awkward first-date robots. Pick an activity where you can be yourself. Now this is the time to mix it up.

If you went out on the town last time, try something more personal and intimate. Or if you slummed it at the local bar (let us hope that this is not the case), take her to a place where she will not get beer splashed on her this time. Show her that you are a well-rounded individual with lots of interests, and she, if she is lucky, might just become one of those interests—confident, not cocky!

## Paying

Traditionally, the one who invited the other picks up the bill. It is a new day and age; once the relationship has been established, try going Dutch (splitting the bill). It is a true testament in determining where a lady's interest stands. If you find yourself contributing more to the relationship without reciprocation, then I'm not saying she's a gold digger … but you can finish the sentence for yourself.

## Romance versus Sex

Intercourse is reserved for the wedded, of course, but if you break the rules, listen up …

It is essential to practice safe sex. There is no worse transgression of good behavior than communicating a sexually transmitted disease. Now that we got that out of the way—some people say you cannot be too forward with women or that one or both of you should be "playing hard to get." In reality, it is a delicate balance. Some women appreciate blunt honesty. If you are playing too hard to get, she might think you are just not interested. If you are complimenting her right and left, she might think you are a freak.

The key is to strike the right tone—throw in a compliment every now and then, but do not make it so obvious that you are falling all over yourself. If you think she is attractive, smart, funny, etc., feel free to tell her. Just do not use every other sentence to mention that you love her eyes, her thighs, etc.

Romance and sex must co-exist—each builds to complement the other. In fact, in a perfect world, you should be so romantically interested in your partner that you both move seamlessly toward nights of more and more intimacy, until sex seems like the most natural thing in the world. Unfortunately, we do not always live in a perfect world, and sex can make matters more complicated than they otherwise would be.

We have all heard of the "walk of shame"—the journey a guy makes the morning after a one-night stand, wearing what he wore last night, hair all messed up and scraggly, as he goes from his lady-friend's condo back to his own. It usually happens right after a conversation that is full of awkwardness and people grabbing at their clothing.

This situation can be avoided entirely if both people involved wait until they genuinely want to have sex with each other, instead of just caving in to make-out urges after tons of drinking. Liquor goggles are not a myth. People do look more attractive when you are drunk. So instead of getting sloshed on dates one and two, go slowly enough that you are sure you like and respect each other as humans. Build the romance first, to make sure there are no regrets the next day.

## Been There, Done That!

Not many men reach the pinnacle of the dating scene. There is indeed an elite group of gentlemen who most guys look up to and most ladies find intriguing. You get to a certain level when you have had it all. You are tired; you are not amused by a big butt and a smile. The things average men desire, you now turn away from. You may be ready for a relationship.

**Wait!** Gentlemen, don't turn the page at the sight of the word *relationship*. The distinguished gentleman relishes the thought of courting the woman with whom he shares extreme compatibility. The foolish gentleman continually seeks temporary pleasures in a wild assortment of women. Being single is a treasured experience. However, chasing skirts and being the bachelor for the remainder of your living leaves no room for being Bereolaesque.

Relationships are not for the faint of heart. They require work and commitment. The C word turns the insides of most men. Commitment can be tough for the gentleman. The amoral gentleman knows what it means to live free and have several women at his disposal. But the contemporary Bereolaesque gentleman knows when its time to leave the playpen and take his seat on the throne with his queen.

## None of Your Friends' Business

Who cares what your friends think about your mate? If she truly is as bad as they say, you will find out soon enough. However, if it is a friend you trust, you might want to ask her a few questions. If there is abuse or danger in a relationship, it is your DUTY as a friend to get involved. It does not have to be directly (to avoid confrontation/altercation).

In the meantime, leave plenty of room for privacy in your relationship. Your bond is special, so protect it. Get to know the person first before inviting the world into your relationship, because the world may very well end it.

*The Gentleman's Gentleman*

## The Gentleman's Gentleman: *Inner Circle*
Gentleman's Club

The *art* of friendship is a unique relationship that requires a special type of *paintbrush*. This camaraderie between a gentleman and his inner circle is unlike any of his other bonds. It is a bond that should never be broken and never be jeopardized. On the other hand, this inner circle usually governs itself on a set of guidelines or a code of ethics that are not disobeyed, and are held in high regard.

Some gentlemen acknowledge this brotherhood with a special handshake, while others get even more carried away, giving their inner circle a title. However you decorate your connection, every gentleman realizes and respects the importance of the bond. Gentlemen, we are indeed Bereolaesque … let us not confuse our inner circle with a childhood gang; we are simply above that!

Generally, each inner circle successfully functions on the basis of love, loyalty, respect, and honor. Gentlemen, this basically means refrain from sleeping with each other's wives, do not speak negatively about members to other people, do not judge but do correct, make yourself available when others are not, and always stick up for one another. Simple rules, right? Well consider yourself a member. A gentleman's club is non-exclusive and is non-hazing. Any and all are welcome. The only requirement is that you are Bereolaesque!

*The Bailout*

## The Bailout: *The Bank of Bereola*

Being Bereolaesque is being healthy, wealthy, and strong … the quest to being Bereolaesque is the journey to all of these things.

Extravagance can become dishonest if carried beyond one's income. Large houses, yachts, and several automobiles are considered symbolic measurements of wealth. This is not a philosophy that we will follow. Real money is expressed in what we do with it, not how we're seen with it.

For a gentleman, stealth wealth and less conspicuous consumption are the order of the day. The contemporary gentleman prefers private pleasures to public swagger, and keeps his personal portfolio privileged. This may be a foreign subject for the flashy, but get used to taking your bank statements off of display. Gentlemen, we are privately wealthy!

The Urban Sophisticate consumes goods that are subtle and not necessarily readable by the general public, but by those in the know. Though our possessions may not always look it, they cost much more than the flashy man's bright suit and cheap jewelry. We focus on quality and limited edition. To be subtle is much more sexy than blatantly obvious.

When your friends are in the same tax bracket you are, there is no need to compete. Competition is for those who are in the process of reaching a goal. Once that goal has been reached, sit back on white sand comfortably with your peers and libations—there is no competition!

A Bereolaesque gentleman is within reason to show off perhaps, but he has subtle ways of showing off his exquisiteness. One-of-a-kind pieces and bespoke suits are certainly some of those ways. Sporting obscure brand names, often without labels and logos, that are only known by those who can afford to know and appreciate their quality is another. If the common man doesn't know what to look for, you have done your job of staying under the radar. And gentlemen, this is the way it should be—it is a subtle yet ironic statement to the public that boldly exclaims: *You can pay for school but you can't buy class ... nor can you buy sophistication!*

A gentleman never flaunts his money. His personal finances are private. His money is his business!

One who is not well off does not "mooch," but pays his own way to the utmost of his ability.

### The Importance of Saving and Investing

Now, it doesn't take a financial advisor to inform you of the importance of saving and investing. It is the philosophy of wealth—*let money make money for you.*

Of course, it is not always that easy. There are three important things to consider before this can happen:

1. **Pay Off Debt:** Debt can be your worst enemy if you allow it to defeat you. Consolidate the monster and get a plan to pay it off a.s.a.p. As gentlemen, you don't want debt following you around, ruining your credibility.

2. **Living Within Your Means:** This means generating a successful income but living like you're a dorm college student. Sacrificing shiny things for a few years can truly assist in you meeting and exceeding short- and long-term financial goals.

3. **Paying You First:** People work hard, get paid, and spend all their money on bills before their paycheck is even posted. We often neglect ourselves and our own interests. We

don't work just to pay bills! This is where the philosophy of paying ourselves comes into play. Each paycheck you receive, deduct a certain percentage for you, and automatically have it placed in a savings account. This does not include your 401K deduction. This may sound like too much icing on the cake, but neglecting yourself when it comes to your money will have you living paycheck to paycheck—*not Bereolaesque!*

## The Art of Negotiation

Never give the exact price of what you are truly willing to spend or sell. Always aim higher, because once a price is set, there is nowhere else for it to go but down.

## The Gentleman in Tough Economic Times

Whatever your world view, it is perhaps fair to say that the increasing complexity of the financial markets demands new ideas and approaches to behavior. Tough times require tough choices. They also require that bad behavior be curtailed and good behavior embraced … especially gentlemanly behavior. When jobs and homes are being lost, there's not much to smile about. Maintaining manners is at the bottom of your priority list as you struggle to simply stay afloat. During these times, it is essential to remain cool. Losing your cool can cause you to lose your judgment—which can cause you to lose your money. These troubles tend to divert our attention away from matters that truly count.

Being Bereolaesque is all about consistency. Regardless of our current situation, we treat everyone politely, and consistently—especially when things are down. When we lose our focus, we lose our manners. When we lose our manners, we lose the essence of who we all strive to be—a contemporary gentleman.

## Gracious Gratuity

### *Tips on Tips*

Display of appreciation is instrumental in being a gentleman. Gratuity is a great way for the gentleman to express his appreciation for services rendered. Whether at the airport, lounge, or your favorite restaurant, always tip very well and discreetly. Eighteen to twenty percent is acceptable, but the level of service can very well increase or decrease that amount.

If the service is horrible, leave a tip but no money—the tip should be a note stating that the service needs improvement.

Be aware that a lot of restaurants include gratuity. Additional gratuity is not necessary in this instance.

*Interlude*

*Touch*

# Women 101: *Essentials for the Gentleman*

**Rule #1:** Women know more than we think.

**Rule #2:** Women test our reactions; they observe, analyze, and judge our every action, expression, word, and gesture. Be mindful of that.

**Rule #3:** Women usually do not express their true anger, so if she looks upset … she is upset.

**Rule #4:** So when women say nothing is wrong, something is wrong.

**Rule #5:** When she says she is ready, she really needs fifteen more minutes. Showing up fifteen minutes early will not solve the problem … she will still need an extra fifteen minutes.

**Rule #6:** A woman prefers to be included. As opposed to asking your lady friend what her plans are, inform her that you would like for her to be a part of your plans.

**Rule #7:** Pay her attention! Women will force emotion out of you if provoked (feel neglected) and an argument may ensue as a result.

**Rule #8:** If she leaves upset, follow her.

**Rule #9:** She may push you away just to see if you are willing to come forward.

**Rule #10:** If she pushes you, hold her closely, tell her you love her, and do not let go.

**Rule #11:** Women create a connection and sense of intimacy through communication; her personal questions are not intended to invade your privacy. Open up.

**Rule #12:** Gentlemen, don't mention other women around her.

**Rule #13:** Do not break her heart, because a good woman scorned is probably gone forever—stop ruining the good ones.

**Rule #14:** When she is not, tell her she is beautiful ... when she is beautiful, tell her she is stunning. A gentleman recognizes beauty is internal.

**Rule #15:** Pay attention! Acknowledge the way her new haircut further defines her bone structure or how sexy her new dress looks on her.

**Rule #16:** If you notice she has put on a few pounds, do not call her fat. Suggest working out together because you want to live more healthily and would like her there for companionship and encouragement; teamwork.

**Rule #17:** Maintain your image as if you were still chasing her; keep yourself up ... do not get too comfortable in the relationship and she will reciprocate.

**Rule #18:** If she is good to you, spoil her.

**Rule #19:** Send her flowers because its Tuesday.

**Rule #20:** Arrange to pick her up from work early to take her to her favorite place.

**Rule #21:** Spend time with her; time can make or break your relationship.

**Rule #22:** When she cries, sometimes it is best to hold her tight and not say a word.

**Rule #23:** Flirt with her.

**Rule #24:** Make her laugh.

**Rule #25:** Let her wear your favorite shirt.

**Rule #26:** Remember special days all year round—set reminders in your PDA.

**Rule #27:** Instead of taking her out, cook for her sometimes.

**Rule #28:** Spray cologne on your shirt she sleeps in and intentionally leave it behind when you go out of town.

**Rule #29:** Rent her favorite movie that you hate and snuggle up with her on a Friday.

**Rule #30:** Be considerate in the bedroom!

**Rule #31:** If you don't, someone else will.

**Rule #32:** Ask her opinion.

**Rule #33:** Do not allow your career/goals to come before what truly matters to you ... her.

*Still a Gentleman*

## Still a Gentleman: *Comfortable Discomfort*
*"Fail until you succeed."*
~~ Luther Jackson

To err is human nature, hence the imperfection of man is certain. The gentleman is aware that life is not detached from flaws, yet the pursuit of perfection remains a daily objective for him. This pursuit is important to every gentleman, because although the goal (perfection) is unobtainable, the journey continuously develops you and makes you better.

In similar contrast to perfection, being Bereolaesque is obtainable. You may say to yourself that declaring something in "similar contrast" is an oxymoron; allow me to explain: Being Bereolaesque is the closest to perfection that man can get, because by definition, it absolutely conforms to the description of an ideal type (*highly appealing and pleasing to the human senses and/or mind; captivating; providing pleasure or delight, esp. in appearance or manner; charming; alluring; attractive*). Now this can be an ideal type of man, woman, food, vehicle, or even a home. The point is that declaring something Bereolaesque insinuates perfection according to a specific person's preferences. Saying that something is perfect for someone suggests that it meets 90 to 99.9 percent of their expectations or needs; the remaining percentage is left for flaws or imperfections.

This book makes it possible for anyone to be Bereolaesque despite flaws; therefore, perfection is obtainable.

The Bereolaesque gentleman understands and accepts his percentage of error (faults), but he is more improved today than he was yesterday, because he is constantly searching within and becoming better. He is going to make mistakes, fumble, and fall short. When he is introduced to your parents and forgets their names, it is okay; he will do better next time. He should not be criticized for it, as he is constantly improving to decrease his error percentage. When he pulls over on the side of the road to rid himself of urine from his uncontrollable bladder (assuming a rest stop is nowhere nearby), he is still a gentleman ... a gentleman with a weak bladder, but a gentleman nonetheless. When he falls, he remembers what tripped him and he gets back up. A gentleman gains wisdom by learning from his and others' failures as well as successes.

In college, there was a buddy of mine that I completely looked up to. He embodied what it meant to be a gentleman. On a spring break, he consumed much too many libations and regurgitated all over my female companion and himself as he collapsed on the ground aimlessly. The next morning, he woke up still a gentleman.

A few years ago, a man had it all; he was barely twenty-five years old, owned his own companies, and was working his way toward his first million. He was the brightest and most mannerly guy you could meet. He got caught in the fast life and blinded by the lights, until the stresses of the cold world got to him. He died still a gentleman.

There was this boy who didn't have much as a child. His parents died at an early age, and he had yet to find himself. He struggled through school and eventually went on to a fine college. He had aspirations beyond anyone's imagination and started on a new journey. Rivals shunned him and called him every name in the book, but he leaned on hope … he woke up in the White House still a gentleman.

A gentleman is who you are, not what accidents occur or what trials get in your way. Yes, we will make mistakes and yes we will fail. Keep failing, gentlemen … fail until you succeed. Because when you are at your lowest low, where else is there to go but up?

Get up, get off the ground, and remember that we won't all be millionaires, we won't all have the best style, and we won't all live to see another day. But while we do exist, let's make our lives matter. Set the example, live a legacy, and let's make every year the year of the gentleman.

Being Bereolaesque allows you to maintain manners and charisma and remain comfortable in uncomfortable situations, all while being true to yourself. Be yourself ... but keep it Bereolaesque!

*The Prayer*

# The Prayer: *Acknowledgment*

The Bereolaesque man acknowledges a higher power. He is aware that blessings do not come from man, and honor shall be given to God. He recognizes that he himself is a rare person created from God's unique mold and there are no duplicates!

The contemporary gentleman accepts God's word as truth and understands that he has been placed on this earth for a purpose greater than himself. He knows that his life is not his own and he is to set examples of good living, unconditional loving, and extreme faith.

The Urban Sophisticate loves people as he loves himself. He accepts people as they are and does not judge. He is patient, even when he would like the other person to hurry up already. He is kind when being mean might seem more productive and more satisfying. He is not jealous of his spouse or of others. He is not pompous or inflated and doesn't think of himself as too important. He is not rude, but rather speaks and acts with courtesy to everyone. He is caring about others before his own self-interests. He does not display his temper, despite his level of anger. He is not brooding and does not hold on to pain. He is not gloating when the other is wrong or makes a mistake. He can withstand any pressure, is always full of hope, and can last through any crisis.

... He is Bereolaesque.

Reach out with compassion and a gentle spirit to all you meet, because they too are carrying a heavy load. We all suffer hardships—be the source of encouragement for people, or at the very least not add to their troubles.

Be Bereolaesque.

*Members Only*

## Members Only: *Summa cum Laude*
### *Unveiling of a Gentleman*


With highest honor,


You have arrived …


You are one of a kind …


You are educated …


You are aware …


You are knowledgeable …


You are the contemporary gentleman!


Congratulations! You have shed your dead skin and come into a new one. You have traded in your old clothes for bespoke suits—you have exchanged the breast milk for bottles of fine champagne and aged wine (legal age). More importantly, you are equipped with the tools necessary to advance in a competitive world, stand out in a positive yet sexy way, and create a legacy for yourself, and generations to come.

Many are called, few are chosen. You are in a class among distinction. You are ready to stare society in the face confidently, and with a new perspective. Just as any expert gives an impression of ease, making their skill seemingly effortless, so too will the Urban Sophisticate.

## You Are a Member Only

Your journey is not over; it is only beginning. You have the responsibility of offering a highly appealing lifestyle of class and distinction in exchange for normalcy. You must educate and uplift, while exposing the gentleman in others, no matter how far hidden. My guys, go make the world just a little bit more Bereolaesque, one gentleman at a time! There will surely be opposition ... make sure you give them a copy of this manual.

We have been awaiting your arrival. You have graced the pages of the Bereolaesque experience. Test this experience on the social scene tonight. Go out and have a good time. You symbolize the art of celebration ... a toast to you, and to being Bereolaesque!

*Enjoy…*

*Finale*

# *Final Words from a Contemporary Gentleman ...*

*"Karma will find you in your most vulnerable moments; exercising good behavior in all situations will secure your karma in these moments."*

*"Your past has passed and this is your now. Your now is what's important. Make wise decisions in the now so your future may be secured."*

*"Never be too prideful to be a janitor."*

*"Make sure you pay attention, because education is what you remember after you close the book."*

*"Sometimes you have to grow apart to grow together."*

*"Oftentimes we are so caught up in the outcome of our prayers that we frequently overlook the fact they have already been answered."*

*"Apologies are meaningless when the action is perpetual."*

*"The more you travel, the smaller the world gets."*

*"If life is a journey, can I find it on MapQuest?"*

*"The final destination pardons the bumpy road."*

*"Smooth seas don't make skillful sailors."*

*"You cannot control every situation, but you can control your reaction to a situation; so in essence, you can control every situation."*

*"Examine thoughts before they turn into feelings, actions, events, and consequences."*

*"Always ask to use a woman's restroom during your first visit to her place. A woman's restroom is one of the most private places in her home; her restroom will tell you a lot about her. If she does not take care of the things you can see, just think about the things you cannot see …"*

*"You cannot accuse a single man of cheating."*

*"A gentleman shall behave as precisely as he would like his children to behave."*

*"Success does not come without sweat."*

*"Do not live life based off circumstance, live life in spite of circumstance."*

*"Do not wait for the world to change, little brother ... change the world."*

*"Etiquette has no place in the bedroom."*

# *Fin!*

*... Now that we've covered you gentlemen, it's time discuss you*

*ladies ...*